A Life Shared

by

James Roose-Evans

PORT MEADOW PRESS

Port Meadow Press
43 Leckford Road, Oxford OX2 6HY
Registered Co. No. 4405635

ISBN 978-1-9998379-5-2

PORT MEADOW PRESS

The growth of love is not a straight line but a series of hills and valleys. I suspect that in every good marriage there are times when love seems to be over. Sometimes these desert lines are simply the only way to the next oasis. Most growth comes through times of trial.

Madeleine L'Engle, *Two-Part Invention*

He has put into my heart a marvellous love.

Psalm 16

A friend is a loved one who awakens your life to the wild possibilities within you.

John O'Donoghue, *Anam Cara*

For Kevin
With gratitude

Prologue

WHEN MY memoir, *Opening Doors and Windows*, was published in 2009 I had to speak at various literary festivals. At one of these I was asked, 'Of all the many achievements in your life which do you rate the highest?' to which I replied without hestitation, 'My fifty-one year relationship with my partner, Hywel Jones,' and with this there was a loud burst of applause.

Hywel was to live another three years until his death, at the age of seventy-six, of a brain tumour. This, however, is not a book about bereavement – though that is part of the story. Rather, it seeks to celebrate a shared life, most of it lived at a time when there were few role models for two men who wanted to spend their lives together, and certainly no legal protection, such as was to come into force some decades later with the passing of a law allowing civil partnerships for same sex couples.

It is difficult for those of the present generation to realise that only a few decades ago not only was homo-sexuality illegal but the fear of exposure forced many into celibacy or sham marriages. Homosexual activities could lead to harsh penalties, imprisonment, or, as in Alan Turing's case, chemical castration by the mandatory administration of estrogen. It was not easy for homo-sexuals to meet – there were some gay clubs and pubs but they were constantly raided by the police. As Jeremy Norman observes in *No Make-Up*, not just the careers of the rich and the famous, but gay people from all walks of life had no protection under the law. Many grew up to fear a sudden knock on the door at night and the house invaded by the police.

It was in 1953 that Sir David Maxwell Fyffe, then Home Secretary, called for 'a new drive against male vice'. Sir John Nott-Bower, who had recently taken over as Commissioner at Scotland Yard, swung into action on a nationwide scale, enlisting the support of police throughout the country to step up the number of arrests for homosexual offences. The view of the law at the time was that homosexuality (curiously this did not apply to lesbians) was a monstrous perversion, deliberately chosen. Homosexual acts were regarded as 'abominable' and 'gross indecency'.

It was also claimed that homosexuality was a symptom of a nation's decadence. In the 1950s British newspapers attacked gay men with a vituperation that harked back to the treatment of Jews in 1930s Germany. A favourite theme of these attacks was the supposed existence of a vast conspiracy. In Britain this was said to extend to the upper reaches of the government, especially the Foreign Office, the institutions of higher learning, and even to British connections overseas.

It is interesting to read the comments of Dr Una Kroll in her book *Bread, Not Stones*. She used to have homosexual men coming to see her in her medical practice because of their fears of being blackmailed, exposed and persecuted for their behaviour. She became increasingly convinced that homosexuality was not an illness but simply a variety of gender identity. After meeting a number of actively homosexual men who had lived as loving and faithful partners for over thirty years – one of whom was a child psychiatrist – she ceased to recommend psychological 'reversion' therapies. She concluded instead that homosexuals were right to regard themselves as a normal, significant minority of the human population with genetic predispositions to same-sex attraction.

The case which attracted the most notoriety in its time was that brought in 1954 against Lord Montagu of Beaulieu, Peter Wildeblood and Michael Pitt-Rivers, each of whom was given a jail sentence for homosexual offences. The case was the subject of considerable controversy and was largely responsible for the Government's decision to set up a Departmental Committee to enquire into the whole question of homosexuality and the laws relating to it.

The Committee was chaired by John (later Lord) Wolfenden after whom the report was named when published in 1957. It recommended the need for a change in the law and its conclusions were backed by the British Medical Association, the Howard League for Penal Reform, the National Association of Probation Officers, as well as by Geoffrey Fisher, then Archbishop of Canterbury.

The Wolfenden Report was not implemented, however, and it was to be another decade before its proposals, permitting sex in private between two consenting adults over the age of twenty-one, became law. This was thanks to the advocacy of Roy Jenkins who, as Home Secretary from 1965–7, and in the teeth of vehement opposition, also oversaw the ending of the death penalty and the laws against abortion. The age of consent was subsequently lowered to eighteen in 1991, and, finally, in 2000 a law was passed equalising the age of consent for both homosexual and heterosexual men at the age of sixteen. Gays slowly began to function openly as couples and mix publicly on equal terms.

And so this is a story of how each of us living through that period coped with the challenges that inevitably arise in any long relationship, above all an unorthodox one: how, for instance, to deal with occasions of sexual infidelity without screaming 'Divorce!' and having recourse to the courts. As gay men we had to make up many of the rules as we went along.

≈ 1 ≈

LOOKING BACK I am amazed at how both ignorant and innocent I was at the age of twenty-two when I went up to Oxford to read English. I did not know what happened sexually between men and women, except in the vaguest sense, and I certainly had no idea of what men did with one another. For young gay men of today this is almost unimaginable, and yet I was not alone in my naïveté. Today, with instant access to online pornography, no one growing up is innocent of the biological facts. What is lacking is knowledge of what love means.

From the start I was an outsider. My mother, like a gypsy, loved to be on the move, for ever yearning to be anywhere rather than her current abode. This meant that I had attended some seventeen schools and lived in many more homes by the time I went to university. Because of this dislocation, of never being in one place long enough to put down roots or form friendships, and especially with the onset of puberty, I felt a strong sense of exile, of not belonging. It is perhaps not surprising that in a sequence of seven children's books I went on to write in my mid thirties the two central characters are called Odd and Elsewhere!

In the fourth volume of the series, *Elsewhere and The Gathering of the Clowns*, Elsewhere says,

> I've had all sorts of adventures. I've been in many places, met many people. Yet I could never feel any

of it was permanent. I enjoyed it but always had the feeling that it could not last. Not in any sad way, but just that things have a way of changing. Nothing ever stays the same. And so I got the feeling that wherever I was I could as easily be elsewhere. That's how I got my name. Odd, too, has always felt the odd man out. I suppose that's why we understand each other so well. And then I always had this feeling that somewhere, elsewhere, something was waiting for me, and that when I found it, I wouldn't any more feel lost. I'd be here and not elsewhere!

C.S. Lewis once remarked that the best children's books are written not so much for children as for the child in one's self, and so in this way they touch a nerve in those who read them. The writing of these books was the healing of a child's wound, of that early experience of separation. How many such wounds, I wonder, go back to childhood and shape our future development?

My sense of drama I owe entirely to my mother whose humours, angers, impulses, laughter and tears were always heightened by histrionics. My roots are deep in hers as were hers in me. Although, as the result of a long and fruitful psychoanalysis which began in my early twenties, I can now contemplate all this at a distance, I am aware that for me, as for many if not most people, our journey begins with our mothers. My father remained at a distance; I rarely received any display of affection, no hugs or embraces, nor sharing of those activities that many boys experience with their fathers.

With the outbreak of war in 1939 our lives changed dramatically. My mother, partly to get away from my father, his drinking and their endless rows, went to work in a munitions factory in Woolwich and I was lodged with a family who lived in Littledean in Gloucestershire. Mrs Pollard had retired from nursing, while her husband had been invalided out of the Army after the First World War because of frostbite in his toes. They had one daughter, Mary, who was studying at the Royal College of Needlework in London. Slowly I became part of the family and learned how to chop wood, saw logs, grow vegetables, cook, sew and darn my own socks. I emptied the slops, fed the hens and collected their eggs. I relished being part of a family, with each day structured, no longer at the mercy of emotional whirlwinds. I began to feel I had a place and a function and I was encouraged to work hard at my studies, so that I rose from the bottom of the class at the Crypt Grammar School in Gloucester, to the top, eventually winning a scholarship to Oxford.

From the window of my bedroom I could see the valley below with the River Severn lying like a glittering scythe and, in the distance, Gloucester Cathedral. Almost the first sound I would hear every morning was the clatter of milk cans as Rob Morgan from the farm below drove up to deposit them for the milkman to collect.

In the holidays I worked on the Morgans' farm, helping out with the haymaking. Often we would have to race against the dark storm clouds in order to get the stack built and covered with a tarpaulin sheet before the rains came. In the summer I took part in the harvest, beginning early while the day was still fresh and cool, and working until late in the evening.

Although Robbie, as his family called him, was two or three years older than I, we soon became good friends so that, whenever I had finished my homework, or during the holidays, I would drop in to help out with whatever jobs needed doing. In winter, observing how his hands would grow cold and chapped as he clenched and released the teats of the cows when milking, I quickly learned how to milk, our heads leaning against the warm flanks of the animals as they munched the hay. Sometimes, if Robbie was up on the Ridge ploughing, he would shout out to me to join him, keeping the tractor running until I was perched beside him.

I envied Robbie his physical strength and his indifference to church or religion, whereas I was riddled with anxieties, scruples and an all-pervading sense of guilt. One summer he and I went off for the whole day, climbing and swimming. On our way home it began to pelt with rain and we ran swiftly down a steep slope, making for a barn by a group of hazel trees. Inside the barn there was the smell of wet earth and dusty hay. Chickens fluffed their feathers, murmuring contentedly as the rain deluged down outside.

I was content just to be there with Robbie but then I became aware of him looking intently at me. He was so close that the odour of his body became mingled with that of the rain-soaked earth and I could feel his breath on my face. I felt his arm encircle my shoulders and then the rain-wet imprint of his lips outlining mine. Our teeth chinked and for one teasing moment our tongues met. It was all over before I realised what had happened. One moment we were close, warm body against body, and the next he had released me. That was all. But then he began to speak in a low voice, almost as though to himself. I let him talk, for rarely did he talk so much, or so vulnerably. I knew that I wanted to hold that moment for ever. It was a profession of friendship coming from one who I had not dared to hope could ever feel towards me as I did towards him. It was as though we had been bonded as brothers by that one kiss.

By the time we returned to the farm it was late and his mother insisted I stay the night, having already sent a message to the Pollards. 'You can just about share Robbie's bed,' said Mrs Morgan, 'and I've put out an old pair of his pyjamas for you.'

In the night I woke to find Robbie fast asleep, lying half across me with one arm over my chest. Listening to his breathing I began to breathe in as he breathed out, making an intertwining pattern of sound, weaving the two of us together. Slowly my breath moved in unison with his until we lay like one person. I felt encased in him, like Ariel in the cloven pine and yet, unlike Ariel, not imprisoned but enveloped in a warm comforting darkness, wrapped in safety, while through the window of the attic bedroom I could see the moon, high up and full, with dark clouds racing across it. It seemed as though we had melted into one another.

What happened in the barn was never referred to again. In due course Robbie married, had children, and put on weight. Yet that memory stays with me. Albert Camus says somewhere that we devote our lives to re-discovering the two or three essential images on which we first opened our eyes. That time with Robbie was a promise of what lay ahead, although I was not then to know it.

From school I went into the Army to do my eighteen months' service, and during that time I became a Catholic convert. On being demobbed I struggled to get work as an actor and then, in the early part of 1949, failing to make any progress, and having had a breakdown which led me into analysis, I went to spend some days at Ampleforth Abbey in Yorkshire where I found myself drawn to the monastic way of life and St Benedict's mixture of prayer, study and manual work. As a result I went to the Abbot to ask if I might enter the Community. He wisely suggested that I should go to St Benet's Hall, Oxford, the house of studies for the English Benedictine Congregation, and take a degree, and 'find out more what kind of a person you are and what kind of people monks are'.

Shortly after my arrival I was given an introduction to David March, an actor at the Oxford Playhouse. He was a deeply committed Catholic, a member of the Third Order of St Dominic, with a wide knowledge of literature, music and Jungian psychology. We began to meet regularly and go to Mass together at Blackfriars, the house for the Dominican Order. In that first autumn of 1949 we took long walks, scuffing through the fallen leaves in Addison's Walk, feeding the deer in Magdalen Park, after which we would cross the road to the tropical swelter of the Botanical Gardens, often finishing up for tea at the Cadena, or returning to his flat to listen to music. Aware that I was testing a religious vocation, he exercised great restraint in his growing affection for me. Then one day, when we were lying chastely on his bed, listening to Vaughan Williams' *Fantasia on a Theme by Thomas Tallis*, he said, 'I love you.'

It was only gradually that I realised what was happening. David was four years older and much more experienced in life, but he was the older brother that, deep down, I knew I had always been seeking. And so, within three months, I moved out of St Benet's and went to live with him. Everyone we knew, including the monks at St Benet's, accepted that we were a couple.

Those were days of such discovery and sharing, long imagined but never before realised. And so it was that slowly, gently, after several months, we moved towards the physical consummation of our love. 'But we must be fraternal in our loving,' said David. 'Our love must not be enclosed, but flow out to others.'

Then, in no time at all, it was spring and then summer. One evening in the Jesuit church, while I was kneeling in contemplation of the Blessed Sacrament, David went to confession. At the edge of my consciousness I was aware that the queue for the confessional was getting longer and more restive. Finally David emerged in a state of distress, having been refused absolution unless he agreed never to see me again. This he had refused to do as he felt that our relationship was 'meant'. He went straight round to Blackfriars and asked to see Father Conrad Pepler. Father

Conrad at once gave him absolution, and then told him that the Catechism was but a rough guide for the faithful who need some rules by which to live. 'A good Catholic,' Father Conrad said, 'should have an informed conscience. He must know what the Church teaches but, in the final analysis, he must follow his own conscience.' In blessing our relationship he said that we must not seek orgasm but if it happened we should not let it burden our conscience: what mattered was that we should learn to love one another. His blessing meant that we were able to bring our love to the altar, there to be nurtured by the Sacraments. Sadly, and in some cases tragically, few of my Catholic contemporaries who were homosexual were so fortunate; instead, they had the painful experience of being rejected by the Church.

David constantly challenged me intellectually. 'Think! Think!' he would say. He taught me discipline, encouraging me to persevere at my studies when, having finally realised I did not have a calling to be a monk, I wanted to leave Oxford and start acting straight away. He taught me that it was important to complete what I had begun, even though a degree was not a necessary qualification for being an actor. Also, through him, both in conversation and watching him at work – for he was a protean actor – I learned much about the craft of acting which, increasingly, I saw was to be my life, having no thought then of being a director.

After I had taken my degree, David and I moved to a one-room attic flat in Belsize Park, London. There were two gas rings on which to cook and we had to share a bathroom on the floor below. I graduated to being a leading man in weekly repertory, where the juvenile character actor, Kenneth Williams, urged me to direct. In 1954 I was appointed Director of the Maddermarket Theatre in Norwich. In that same year I met the great American dancer, Martha Graham. I recall vividly every performance of her London season. Determined to learn more about this new form of theatre, modern dance, I wrote to various institutions in America and, as a result, in 1955 I was invited to join the Faculty of the Juilliard School of Music in New York. There I was given a studio, a composer, several dancers, musicians and singers, and invited to experiment with exploring the relationship between dance, music and drama. I called the course *Theatre of the Imagination.*

One afternoon, shortly before I left, David observed quietly, 'You are beginning to find your own wings. Soon you will not need me.' I was shocked since I could not imagine such a thing: he was my anchor. Yet he foresaw quite clearly that being in another culture would be the making and maturing of me, and that I would come back a changed person. He would be proved right. When I did return things between us were different.

One evening, boxed up in our one-room attic flat, with its gas rings and shared bathroom, David suddenly cried out like an animal in pain, 'Don't you love me any more?!' It wasn't that I was having dalliances elsewhere, but I had matured and was now more focused on my theatre work and less dependent on him.

Faced with the intensity of his emotion and not

knowing how to respond, I went to call on my friend, the writer Eleanor Farjeon, who, disturbed by what I told her of our claustrophobic life together in that one small room, immediately offered us at a peppercorn rent a tiny three-roomed cottage that she owned in Perrins Court, off Hampstead High Street. It had once been the village sweetshop, and before that the cobbler's. It had a toilet but no bathroom; and so for baths we would take our towels and go across to Eleanor's in Perrins Walk. Small though it was, it at least gave us a room each.

We lived there for about three years. But David began to seek liaisons with other men. Living under the same roof, and in such close proximity, became increasingly painful – especially when his lovers stayed over. It was this that led me one night, when he was away, to visit the *King William IV*, a popular gay pub round the corner. I had never before been to a gay pub – but now I was driven by loneliness to make a visit.

≈ 2 ≈

THE PLACE was crowded. Standing ill at ease among a crush of bodies I heard a camp voice behind me saying, 'This is my first time here. I've come up from Brighton. Do you come here often?'

I made no answer and did not turn around.

'You are *very* difficult. Here I am doing my best to talk to you and you don't even answer!'

Suddenly I began to laugh and it was at this moment that I saw across the crowded room a young man with brown eyes watching this encounter with amusement.

'Why are you laughing?' said the Brighton Belle. 'I think you're very rude!' And of course I was, but I was feeling so awkward, not knowing how to cope. I turned and saw the brown eyes laughing too. There was an immediate spark of recognition and as he passed me I said, 'Would you like a cup of coffee?'

Never before had I done anything like this, so direct and spontaneous. We went back to Eleanor's cottage in Perrins Court, talked, and then to bed.

His name was Hywel Jones and we were to be together until his death in 2012. If marriages are supposedly made in Heaven they are also, it seems, made in gay pubs. Had I not gone there on that particular evening Hywel and I might never have met. It turns out it was also his first visit to the *King William IV*. Was there a destiny at work here? Who can tell why some find the perfect partner and some never do? It remains a mystery.

Short, his shoulders slightly rounded as though from carrying a yoke, with shaggy black hair and glowing brown eyes, his was a gypsy face with the bone structure of Rudolf Nureyev. He came from North Wales. Having been demobbed after National Service, he had managed to secure a room in London in return for operating the switchboard in a block of flats managed by his cousin, Edie Morris.

One morning the phone rang and Hywel, at his most puckish, replied, 'Buckingham Palace. I am afraid Her Majesty is unavailable as she is busy cleaning windows.' The caller, who was the owner of the flats, was not amused! As a result Hywel was put on cleaning duty but that didn't suit him any better. On one occasion he left the hoover running while he went out for tea. When he came back it had eaten a hole in the carpet. Having worked in the library in Dolgellau before doing his military service in the army, he then got a job at the Institute for Legal Studies in Bloomsbury. We would often meet during his lunch break, by the statue of Gandhi, and eat our sandwiches together.

On occasion Hywel had a very bad stammer which caused his lips to become distorted. At such moments he was like a mountain stream, bubbling with excitement, his eyes glowing, his mouth and throat trembling in his eagerness to express himself. I was, therefore, startled when, one day, he suddenly stammered out, 'Jim, what I really want to do is to become an actor. If it weren't for this stammer I know I could!' My heart sank and I thought, 'Oh no!' But in fact, over time, he was to prove a natural and highly original actor.

From the start I knew that Hywel was 'the one', but because he was nine years younger and had never been in a relationship before, I realised that I had to exercise great patience. He was temperamentally more cautious than me and always very down to earth. One day as we sat on Hampstead Heath he said, 'One lives from day to day, one day at a time. Otherwise one starts building up expectations and then one gets disappointed. I am glad we have met and if you have the patience and the desire to continue I will give it all I can, and we'll leave the rest to time and, thank God, the unknown future!'

In those early stages of our relationship I wanted to learn more about Hywel, his roots and his background; and so, in that first summer, I decided to make a solitary pilgrimage to his village of Llangynog in the Berwyn Mountains, hitch-hiking all the way – which I knew he would be doing the following week in order to visit his parents.

I first hitched a lift to Dolgellau to visit the library where Hywel had worked after leaving school while waiting to do his military service. A temporary wooden hut with cell-like compartments of books, its windows looked down on the grey town which, only the day before, had been visited by the Duke of Edinburgh. There I met Elwyn Griffiths and his assistant Jeannie. His face lit up when I mentioned Hywel.

'He came here direct from school. He was a bright boy, very quick at learning. He soon picked it up. Now he's a man he should take the final examinations and qualify as a librarian. He went into the Army and said he would come back here but then he wrote saying he was going to stay in London. Next I heard was when he wrote to me for a reference for a job at the Institute of Advanced Legal Studies.' He smiled wryly. 'We never heard if he got the job! And he's never been back. We wondered if it was a girl interested him there? What's he like with the girls?'

At this Jeannie laughed.

'We thought perhaps he had met someone,' continued Mr Griffiths. 'He's such a cheerful person is Hywel, full of fun, a good chap. How did you meet him? … Oh, I thought by the way you speak that perhaps you were a speech therapist and had met him that way. How's his stammer? He used to go red in the face with it. Then when he was in the Army they sent him to a psychiatrist or something and it was much better.'

He departed to deal with someone's query and now Jeannie began to talk, shyly at first, on the defensive, as she stood sticking labels onto a pile of books.

'I wrote to Hywel but he never answered. We used to fight and have terrible rows – terrible! And he'd not speak for an hour. And then suddenly it would be all over. He used to cheek me something rotten. But he could do no wrong for Mr Griffiths. He was Mr Griffith's pet. I'd tell Hywel off about something, perhaps to put away some books, and then Mr Griffiths would come along and say, "What are you doing, Hywel? Oh, leave those!" In the end I said to Mr Griffiths, "I'm never going to tell Hywel to do anything!" Finally it got so bad that I had it out with Mr Griffiths in that room – a terrible row it was! When Hywel went off to the Army we teased him and had him in the back room with his shirt off and we stamped him with every stamp in the library!'

Through the windows I gazed down at the small town and tried to imagine Hywel looking out on such a rainy day, sorting books, drinking tea, laughing and wondering what lay ahead for him. Then I heard Jeannie talking in Welsh to someone and I thought of her remark, 'He never came back.' How warmly, with a touch of asperity, yet sadly too, they had spoken of him. He was indeed gone from their valley.

The next morning it was raining as I set out for Llangynog. A car stopped to give me a lift and we drove up onto high moorland covered with bracken, beyond which the Berwyn Mountains were swirling with mist. Finally we came to the last ridge, Milltir Gerig. There, below us, lay Hywel's valley, the valley of the Rhiwarth, and I knew that was where I must get out and travel the rest of the way on foot. On either side the mountains rose steeply. A roaring sound revealed a steep waterfall cascading recklessly down, then flowing along the floor of the valley. Finally I entered the village, with its disused slate quarry and iron mines, and the single rail track laid down in the prosperous 1880s which had been in use right up until just a few years earlier. There were two inns, a church, three chapels, a post-office, and a general store run by Mr Griffiths. I booked in at the Tanat Valley Hotel, my room facing the crossroads at the centre of the village. It was still raining.

The following afternoon, the rain having stopped, I went to the Annual Flower Show held in the Memorial Hall. Trestle tables were set out with vases of specimen flowers, mixed posies, and country flowers – the latter being the children's entry. There were also tables loaded with choice vegetables: huge polished onions, their stems cut short; giant marrows, cucumbers and swedes. I chatted with Mr Edward Evans, the postman, who was also a chapel elder. From him I learned that not only was the annual Eisteddfod held in the hall for children, but that a first-rate amateur theatre company from nearby Llanrhaeadr-ym-Mochnant regularly performed there, while a professional company, the Midland Players, visited each year. I wondered if this was how the idea of becoming an actor had first been planted in Hywel.

Years later, his sister Mair told me how he used to enjoy visiting two spinster sisters for a gossip, and on one occasion, as a bet, they dared Hywel – he was then sixteen – to dress up as a tramp and go round the village begging for a sandwich and a cup of tea. He began at the house of the local music teacher who sent him off with a flea in his ear. He then went to the local council houses where an Irish woman made him tea and a sandwich, but he blew it all by bursting out laughing!

The next evening, being Sunday, I went to the Primitive Methodist Chapel, which Hywel used to attend with his family. For my benefit one hymn was sung in English and after the sermon Mr Edward Evans gave out the notices in Welsh. Suddenly he was speaking in English and saying, 'We have a visitor among us. I don't know his name but I met him yesterday in the village asking where to stay, and then he asked me what time chapel was this evening. I hope he enjoys his stay with us.' This was the same Edward Evans, as Hywel told me later, who, when serving in the village shop, always had a fag in his mouth with an inch of ash at one end. As children they would watch with fascination as he cut a slice of cheese or some rashers of bacon, waiting for the moment when he coughed, and the ash would fall onto the food!

I would like to have stayed longer but I had to return to England, to direct a production of André Birabeau's play, *The Head of the Family*, at the Belgrade Theatre, Coventry, with the young Michael Crawford in the lead. Waiting for me at the theatre was a letter from Hywel.

Dearest Jimmie, I have just returned to London from Llangynog and part of the time has been wonderful. On Thursday I hitched a lift with a rather lonely, tired but kind furnishing representative. I arrived home about half past seven and my mother was in a very good mood. We talked and gossiped late into the night and it made me very happy to see her so well, almost like old times, before she started getting these depressions and having electric shock treatment in an attempt to cure her. On Friday afternoon I went fishing and caught two trout but got soaking wet. I had taken off my trousers so that I could wade in the deep parts, and then I lay on the bank and fell asleep in the sun.

I knew from what Hywel had already told me that a great outdoor sport in the village was poaching for fish and rabbits, and how there were two methods for catching fish. The first was called 'tickling', at which he was very adept, catching the fish by hand. During warm summer weather and dressed in an old pair of trousers and old boots on the feet as protection from sharp stones, he would wade in the river, feeling for fish under all the large stones or the roots of trees growing on the banks. 'You have to move your hand very slowly,' he explained, 'and when you discover a fish you bring your other hand round to block the exit. Then, holding it gently with both hands, you bring it out and back home for supper!'

In the letter he continued,

After tea my mother told me of all the people who have died in the village in the past twelve months. People I have known all my life, figures evocative of childhood. Even a wild cat who has haunted the farmyard and outbuildings for years has disappeared. She never really became friendly, and I can remember coming upon her in the hay-loft in the dark, her eyes hostile, like sparkling jewels.

But the wonderful peace and quiet after dark is still here. We must try and spend some time together in Llangynog, Jimmie; because after dark the mountains and the stillness have a kind of spiritual quality, and I am sure it would help us to share it together. I came back a day earlier because this morning my mother was back on the trail and because when that happens nobody can say or do anything to help her.

Some months later I moved out of Perrins Court and

went to live in Eleanor Farjeon's garden room at the back of Church Row. David and I remained friends. He subsequently formed another relationship which lasted forty years or more. Later, he also acted with Hywel in my production of *Oedipus* at the Hampstead Theatre Club, in which Svetlana Beriosova played Jocasta.

Eleanor's garden room, musty with the smell of old books, was to prove a haven at this time of great change. One evening I looked up to see Hywel's face peering through the window, grinning. Eleanor then appeared with bananas and cake and was introduced. We talked about schools, the eleven plus examination, and our different upbringings: Hywel's on the farm, and Eleanor's bohemian background. Then she took Hywel round the sights, to the upper garden and through her house, after which we sat in her kitchen over tea – 'Large cups, last thing at night, on a bare table, this is what we do at home,' said Hywel.

Back in the Garden Room, I wrote in my journal:

There is the smell of earth, the sound of distant rattling trains, an owl hooting. And now, with Hywel departed, alone and yet not alone, the door open to the night with the fresh smell of dew on the grass and mist, that sharp smell as of autumn. The silence seeps into one's being.

More and more I wanted to live with Hywel, to share our lives at a deeper level. And yet, at the same time, part of me was scared of making such a commitment to someone I had yet to get to know well. It was, in fact, to be two years before we started living together. But, as the months went by, we shared so much happiness and I sensed that we recognised each other's needs. One evening in November we took a walk in the fog. Lights glowed in houses in the tea-time dusk, everything silent after a recent fall of snow. Hywel was wearing my overcoat. 'I'll borrow it for the winter!' he joked. We went to watch the model boats on Whitestone Pond by Hampstead Heath, boys and youths crowding at the sides. One of them stuck a sparkler in his boat and as it travelled in circles so it scattered sparks, casting a warm glow on the watching faces.

We went to hear Rosalyn Tureck play *The Goldberg Variations* at the Festival Hall and I thought, if one really loves another person for what and who they are in themselves, as well as what they mean to one's self, and if there is a true sense of kinship, then there is nothing one will not forgo for the sake of this thing, knowing that 'the course of true love never did run smooth'. Whatever the outcome, the kindling glow was there. That was enough.

Even though I despaired sometimes that Hywel would ever be in love with me, I knew it was important that he feel free, 'otherwise you might lose me altogether, Jim. I want to be in love and some day I shall meet someone and I don't want to hurt you.' All this I foresaw and accepted, and yet I continued to feel that we had something special between us.

In no time at all it was Christmas and Hywel went home to Llangynog. On the morning of his return, he wrote: 'It was wild with wind and the clouds flying low, then the sun rising at dawn; it made me think of Eli Jenkins' morning prayer in *Under Milk Wood*, "by mountains where King Arthur dreams" – the mountains seemed so timeless. You must spend one Christmas in Llangynog.'

A few days later we were invited to an unexpected and delayed Christmas gathering at Eleanor Farjeon's, together with the actor Denys Blakelock – just the four of us. At one point Hywel recited the whole of Eli Jenkins' prayer, the first time he had ever done anything like this in public. He spoke it quietly, without any hesitations, and at one point, being so caught up in the poem, lifted his head as though facing the oncoming winds.

Once, searching for a word, he turned instinctively, trustingly, to me, his dark eyes glowing, waiting for me to prompt him. He seemed suddenly to have grown more relaxed, and there was a greater trust in our relationship, a mutual respect, affection and need, and I marvelled at all this. 'Mae wedi bod yn bore dda – It's been a good day!' said Hywel afterwards.

On New Year's Eve we went to the Welsh Pub in Gray's Inn Road to celebrate. Everyone had a tankard in one hand and a cigarette in the other as they sang, their voices climbing higher and higher with enormous vigour, while one man stood on the counter to conduct. Gradually, the atmosphere began to deteriorate; but still they called for the old favourites: *Sospan fach, Cariad,* and others. At one moment Hywel and I stood with our foreheads together in search of a half-remembered melody. There seemed to be an invisible chord, as well as a cord, connecting us so that when, at midnight, everyone turned to kiss their partner, Hywel moved spontaneously to kiss me and then, realising where we were, laughed and said 'Girls only!'

As we made our way back he would punctuate his journey with an upheld arm, the gesture almost Whitmanesque, as he hailed people across the street, 'A Happy New Year to you, my dear!' How easily he goes out to people, I thought, so that at King's Cross, seeing two men fighting in a doorway and a woman trying to separate them, he, hands in his pockets, collar turned up, shoulders hunched, his head thrust forward, laughingly went up to them and made a joke of it. They turned against him, swearing and threatening to beat him up. He started to argue, insouciant, like a grinning urchin, and I murmured, 'Come on, Hywel – keep walking and don't look back!'

We awoke to a crisp but sunny morning. January 1st 1959. For a moment Hywel stood at the open window looking out at the new day and the new year. Quietly, without forcing it into words we were, I knew, happy in each other.

~ 3 ~

ONCE THE NEW YEAR had settled in I encouraged Hywel to have lessons with Joyce Bird, a teacher of the Alexander Technique, and it was this that eventually enabled him to overcome his stammer. The Technique is a system devised by F. Mathias Alexander in the 1890s to help people become aware of the unconscious patterns of behaviour which create postural problems, vocal damage or pain. Alexander realised that many vocal problems are caused by over-tension of the neck muscles. Today the Alexander Technique is taught in many parts of the world and is especially beneficial to musicians, actors and athletes.

One day, walking home, Hywel said gently, 'Do you realise it's almost a year since we met?' He then told me of a dream he had had: 'I dreamt I received a telegram saying you had died, and I cried as I have never cried before. Then I heard you were not dead at all. Later, I went into a large building – was it a church? – and a man was preaching, saying, "You must think beautiful thoughts." I felt elated.'

Later that month he crashed through the door after midnight, flushed and glowing, bursting with excitement at having thrown over his job at the Institute. He was going, he said, on holiday for five weeks with his land-lord, the actor Hugh Manning, and his partner. At first I was desperately jealous, but then realised how important it was for him to assert his independence and that it would be a time of discovery for him.

On his return we went to see John Gielgud's one-man Shakespeare recital. At the end the house-lights were lowered because of the continued applause and Gielgud, shaken by emotion, spoke with great sadness the lament from *Cymbeline*: 'Fear no more the heat of the sun, nor the furious winter's rages: Golden lads, and girls, all must, as chimney sweepers come to dust.' Then, with a final upward fling of his arm, he was gone.

On the way home, Hywel and I began to bicker. The next day I collapsed into a blank of fatigue and realised I needed a few days alone. It seemed as though we had reached an implacable impasse and I didn't know what to do.

A few days later he dropped by. 'What's the matter?' he asked. For a moment he leant his head on my chest – and then broke down, sobbing violently.

'I haven't cried for years,' he said. Gradually he relaxed and began to talk. 'I thought that all communication between us was blocked,' he said. 'There will always be communication between us,' I replied, and he answered, 'I hope so.'

I was reminded how, on another occasion, having had too much to drink, he had broken down in my arms sobbing, 'I can't see you! I can't see you!' and it was then that he spoke again of how he wanted to be something, to belong, to be an actor.

The following year, 1960, I went to direct all six plays at the Pitlochry Festival Theatre in Scotland. Hywel was engaged to join the company as an assistant stage manager and to play small parts. Knowing now the direction in which he wanted to go, he was like an arrow released. There was a glitter of excitement in his eyes, his lips grew firmer, he began to put on weight (when we first met it was like sleeping with a skeleton, he was so under-nourished) and, as a result of his Alexander lessons, his back straightened. He glowed like a robin in winter, imbued with a new energy and zest for life, happy and contented. His first small role was in a new play, *Napoleon in Love*, by R.F. Delderfield. In the opening scene he had to play a prisoner who is being questioned by Napoleon. When the Emperor asked him his name Hywel had to reply, 'Staps!' Never once did the 's' sound trip him up, and he went on to play larger parts in the other plays, including a late night production of Harold Pinter's *The Dumb Waiter*.

One week-end at Pitlochry I was overwhelmed with a feeling that I needed to get away and to stay somewhere I didn't know anyone. I managed to find a small country inn in a remote location. And it was there, in the middle of the night, that suddenly all my demons rose up so that I seemed surrounded by griffons, panthers, hyenas, thunder-hoofed horses and strange hybrid monsters. My relationship with Hywel was by now two years old yet still in some ways unresolved. From the start I had always been one jump ahead, knowing he was 'the one'; but my ardour had almost burned itself out in that first year of wooing, so that when, at Pitlochry, Hywel had one day said 'I love you', I had almost given up hope that it might be so.

But the fire had only burnt low and from that time onward the richest part of our relationship began – full of wonder, challenge, discovery, frustration and contentment. And yet I was frightened at the thought of committing myself to taking a flat and sharing it with him. At close quarters would we survive such intimacy? During that long night of dreams I faced all these fears and in the morning rose, tired but refreshed, ready to face my inner demons and see everything in perspective.

Hywel left Scotland briefly to travel to London for an audition at the London Academy of Music and Dramatic Art. To his delight he won a place – and later secured a grant from the London County Council to pay for his studies. And when I travelled down each weekend to Birmingham to appear as the presenter on *Sunday Break*, a religious television programme for young people, a stream of his letters would accompany me.

One such letter began, 'Dearest and beloved Jimmie, When I saw your card this morning the pain of missing you jolted me like a knife thrust. But, as with all things, it passed.' He then went on to describe how late one evening he and Margo Ford, my assistant director, had gone for a walk around the Loch and came to where the boats were, 'and of course we had to go in one! It was wonderful on such a night, the surface of the water as calm and ominous as black marble. We rowed for a long time – the mountains and the over-hanging trees dimly visible on the banks and reflected in the water. We were guided, or liked to think we were, by a solitary evening star.'

I have been asked on a number of occasions whether as a couple we ever experienced homophobic behaviour. The answer is a simple no. In London, of course, we moved in a world of writers and actors and artists. But even when we had a home in Wales, deep in the border country, we always seemed welcome wherever we went – though one is not to know what might be said behind one's back!

Just once, however, we had a glimpse of what many gay men must have experienced. In the first two months at Pitlochry I lived in a hotel and always, on his afternoon off, Hywel would visit me and we would go to bed. On one occasion we heard footsteps approaching and then a knock on the door. We lay quite still. Whoever it was then tried the handle of the door but fortunately I had locked it. Then we heard the footsteps going away. We quickly dressed and Hywel slipped away. Clearly someone had noticed his regular visits. Colin Spencer in his book, *Which of us Two?* writes: 'We are inclined to forget now the appalling effect on young homosexuals … We were outlaws. We grew up to fear the police. I do not exaggerate. When there can be a knock on the door at night, the house invaded by uniformed men who then examine the way you live and the condition of your bed linen, you exist in a social tyranny ruled by bigots.'

At the end of the Pitlochry season we returned to London for the commencement of Hywel's studies at LAMDA. He discovered an attic flat in Belsize Park Gardens – where we were to end up living for just over fifty years. The rent was £6 a week but it was advertised as suitable only for girls. When he asked the owner of the house why this was so, she explained that we would have to share the bathroom and toilet on the floor below with four young women and 'you know how long they can take!' However, we decided to move in; we couldn't afford anywhere else, even though sometimes it meant sitting on the stairs dying for a pee, while the girls were doing their hair or washing their smalls.

There was a small room at the back with a gas cooker in one corner, but no kitchen, and a corridor that led to the front room. For the first ten years or so we had hardly any furniture and slept on mattresses. Hywel took various jobs – doing newspaper rounds, driving the school bus, even for time being a telephonist, while I was either on the dole or earning a pittance reading scripts for Armchair Theatre at Associated Rediffusion Television. Then the opportunity came for all the tenants in the house to purchase the freehold from the Church Commissioners. We bought ours for £2,000, helped by friends.

It was then that Hywel displayed an unexpected flair, as he began to burrow into the eaves of the attic roof, creating first a bathroom and then, gradually as and when there was enough spare cash, a kitchen, a central bedroom for himself, and from it a ladder leading up to a loft which became my bedroom. Later on, as a pledge of confidence, long before civil partnerships were even dreamed of, I gave my share of the flat to Hywel so that even if we did break up he would have a home of his own. Being a Cancerian, the nest was very important to him.

～ 4 ～

ONE DAY I was sitting in a coffee shop having a chat with an actor friend who suddenly said, 'Why don't you start a theatre here in Hampstead?'

'But where?' I replied.

'What about the Moreland Hall next to the Everyman Cinema, up the road there? It belongs to the Hampstead Parish Church and is part of their school.'

The next day I made an appointment to see the vicar and booked the hall for a series of dates over the coming year, Friday to Sunday evenings, when the place was not in use. I then paid a visit to the offices of the *Hampstead and Highgate Express* in Perrins Court, and announced what was planned. The following week, in headlines on the front page were the words: HAMPSTEAD TO HAVE ITS OWN NEIGHBOURHOOD PLAYHOUSE!

Stalls, manned by actors and actresses were set up in the High Street and the first play was announced – a very Welsh affair – *Siwan* by the Welsh poet Saunders Lewis, translated by the Welsh writer Emyr Humphreys, with Siân Phillips and Robert Marsden in the leading roles. At one point in rehearsal Siân asked Robert, 'Are we going to be paid?' and he replied, 'No, Jimmie hasn't got a penny!'

Despite a successful first season we were not allowed to extend our hire of the hall on the grounds that we were getting in the way of the Cubs and Brownies. Then, in December, Hampstead Borough Council gave £7,000 for the shell of a prefabricated building, designed by Anthony Gough, on a site at Swiss Cottage owned by the Council, while I was left to raise £10,000 for the seating, lighting, sound equipment and other furnishings. And so, at long last, while the country still waited for its National Theatre, 'London's first civic theatre', as the press chose to describe it, opened on 16 December 1960 on a site that later was to include a swimming pool and library designed by Sir Basil Spence.

It happened to be one of the worst winters on record, with deep snow and blizzards. There was no money to advertise and few people knew where the new theatre was. By January 13th newspapers were carrying reports that 'The Hampstead Theatre Club has been hit by bad weather and is £6,500 in the red.'

Weeks of snow, no subsidy, lacking funds for adequate publicity, it looked as though the theatre would have to close. I was summoned before the Hampstead Borough Council to explain our failure. It was at this point that Max Rayne (later Lord Rayne and a subsequent Chairman of the National Theatre) came to our rescue and cleared all the debts.

The Hampstead Theatre Club was the first full-time fringe theatre in the UK to have its own premises, but unlike the fringe theatre of the 1970s onwards it received no grants. We lurched from one financial crisis to another for seven years until finally the Arts Council gave us a grant. We were a minimal staff, unlike the Hampstead Theatre today, and we existed (I should say subsisted) on minimal salaries – I was paid £10 a week. We owed so much to the support of local volunteers who acted as programme sellers, ushers and coffee bar attendants. It was solely the sense of passion and belief in what we were doing that made it all possible.

Our chief frustration in those early years lay in trying to get the critics to cover our openings. Without the means to advertise, we were entirely dependent on their reviews for publicity, and the Society of West End Theatre Managers refused to release dates of forthcoming openings, as a result of which our first nights often clashed with those in the West End.

It was at our lowest point, with audiences often little larger than the size of the casts, that I decided to mount a revival of Noel Coward's *Private Lives*. Coward's reputation at that point was waning but I was convinced that it was a work of depth as well as a masterpiece of wit and style. Our production was to result in a major Coward revival which Coward himself subsequently referred to as 'Dad's renaissance'.

While we were in rehearsal I wrote to Harold Hobson, then the leading drama critic of *The Sunday Times*, begging him to come, urging London's need for such a small theatre. I added in block capitals, WE NEED YOUR SPACE! As a result he came to the first night and wrote the review of a lifetime which ended with these words:

The best work in modern drama is being done in the genre of intimate plays for small theatres. Paris has plenty of playhouses for them – the Lutèce, the Poche, the Théâtre du Tertre; but London none. But here in Hampstead is just what we need. This tiny, attractive, simple theatre is accurately in the spirit of Obaldia, Arrabal, Genet, Duras. In Mr Roose-Evans it has a director of unusual sensibility and knowledge.

It is, of course, early days yet; but in my opinion the conditions are such that this Hampstead theatre could conceivably do in England work of the value and fame of the Oeuvre or the Vieux Colombier in France. The trumpets are blowing for other causes than that of Mr Roose-Evans; but I hope that amidst the din his clear, pure call will be heard. His venture interests me more than anything I have encountered in the theatre of this nature since I first heard of Marguerite Duras's *The Square*.

The other critics followed suit and the production transferred to the West End. Suddenly the Hampstead Theatre Club was the talk of the town.

～ 5 ～

WHILE ALL this was happening, Hywel and I were learning to live together. 'What terrible forces we unleash in one another!' I wrote in my journal. 'We have had our second fierce argument in five days and these arguments are in danger of becoming a pattern of our life together.' Usually they would begin with something I had said, which Hywel would then challenge, his riposte growing in intensity into sweeping generalisations until he seemed to be attacking me personally, leaving me feeling as though I were fighting for my life! At such times we seemed locked in a terrible embrace: the whole fabric of my existence, who I was, what I had grown to be, would be challenged.

It was as though I were being torn up by the roots. It may sound melodramatic, and to some extent it was, yet for Hywel these conflicts often seemed no more than teeth-cutting, like a puppy gnawing at a bone. And then, having aroused me, he would nonchalantly walk away! I kept having to remind myself that he was nine years younger and was often using me as a sounding board, testing out his own ideas. Time and again I would fall into the trap when, faced with the extreme emotionalism of his arguments, I would try to respond logically, to stop him shooting off at tangents. What wild darkness was released in him at such moments? I had to learn to help by not getting emotionally involved. Hywel had once described to me how he and another boy, walking home from school, would suddenly start fighting, 'and it would get out of hand,' said Hywel, 'until suddenly I stopped and thought: What are we fighting about?'

Slowly, and helped by the practice of meditation, I learned to anticipate these moments and step aside. But sometimes I would be caught out. On one occasion, Hywel was lying on his bed, by the side of which was a small pine chest of drawers and on top of it a plaster replica bust of Hermes that meant a lot to him. In my rage and frustration at the way he was attacking me, I picked up the bust and smashed its head violently against the wall. Hywel cowered back, saying, 'I shall never forgive you for that!'

He did, of course, forgive me. But, as the broken pieces of Hermes fell around us, I was shaken by the realisation of how easily murder can happen. And what shook me further was that earlier in the year, Kenneth Halliwell, in a rage, had murdered his partner, Joe Orton the playwright, smashing his skull so violently that Joe's brains were splattered over the walls and ceiling.

Years later I found a bust, carved in white marble, of the young Augustus Caesar, which I bought and gave to Hywel. After that episode no more such incidents occurred.

It is, as Rilke observes, 'good to love because love is difficult'. He goes on:

> For one human being to love another is perhaps the most difficult task that has been entrusted to us, the ultimate task, the final test and proof, the work for which all other work is preparation. This is why young

people, who are beginners in everything, are not yet capable of love: it is something they must learn. With their whole being, with all their forces, they must learn to love.

It is easy to fall in love, but being in love demands work. The challenge of all committed relationships, as we were both beginning to learn, was to allow the freedom of individual growth within the container of the relationship, while slowly bits of the ego are being chipped away.

During Hywel's time at LAMDA there was some concern about his stammer, although by then it had almost disappeared. The teacher who best understood him, Freda Hodgson, wrote:

His performance as the Pope in an early play by Peter Ustinov was incredibly revealing in its spiritual depth. He did not know how revealing, indeed he has this unique quality, he knows not what he knows. He has an inspiration, a great light, a tremendously warm and co-operative personality and a hundred per cent integrity. His difficulty at present is the co-ordination of speech. There is a hiatus between what he is going to say and the motivation, almost a limbo of nothingness and yet, out of this limbo, there comes his gift of being able to tune in to the inarticulate moment. He has a very deep humility, you know that every thing you say goes in and this humility is linked with great patience on his part.

It was at this period that we acquired a tri-coloured Cavalier spaniel. We called him Titus. He came to us as a puppy from a breeder and had to be trained. I had just commissioned, on behalf of Hampstead, an adaptation for the stage of Frederick Rolfe's novel *Hadrian the Seventh* from Peter Luke who was then Head of Drama for Associated Television. His script arrived and, having to go out, I inadvertently left both the script and the puppy in the same room. When I returned the floor was covered with torn scraps of Peter Luke's play, like a snowstorm of paper.

Then, on 12 January 1963 at half past four, the phone rang with a message for me that five girls were waiting at the theatre to be auditioned: Had I forgotten?

I dashed out of the house, followed excitedly by Titus who had not had a run that day. There was deep snow everywhere – snow so deep in fact that there was no traffic and so I didn't bother about using a lead. We passed Hywel returning from the shops and Titus started to follow him but I whistled and he came racing after me, his ears flying behind him, his feather tail uplifted. At that moment, quite unexpectedly, a car appeared as he raced across Lancaster Grove. The car didn't stop. I cried out, 'Hywel! Hywel!' as I went to pick up Titus. His head flopped and his eyes were filled with blood. I cried out to some workmen nearby, 'Is there a car? I must get him to a vet.' At that moment Hywel came up to me and Titus' tail twitched. Although it was only a muscular reaction it seemed like a farewell gesture. I knew he was dead. His body lay in my arms, heavy and relaxed, like that of a lover. Hywel gave out strange cries as we walked back along Lambolle Crescent to our flat. We laid Titus in a box in the garden under the trees, the ground too frozen to dig a grave.

'It was my fault!' sobbed Hywel. No, I said, it just happened. For an hour we sat in the front room, drained. Looking into Hywel's eyes it was as if he, too, had died. He had been so especially close to Titus, who would always lie on his bed. At one point we went into the kitchen and saw his empty basket and food bowl. We couldn't eat our dinner and didn't even attempt it. He was so beautiful and now he was dead. Torn between his love for each of us, he had come racing towards me and on that leap was killed.

The next morning when the front door bell rang, I ran down the five flights of stairs to let in Hywel, who had gone out without his key. And then it hit me: always when the bell rang Titus would leap up and cascade down the stairs to greet Hywel or me.

We ordered another Cavalier spaniel. It seemed the only thing to do. Lying in bed, weeping, Hywel said, 'I'm glad we've got another. That's right.' And at intervals he continued to murmur, 'Poor Titus!'

As London's first fringe venue the Hampstead Theatre was overwhelmed by writers and their agents wanting us to stage their work. We also mounted revivals of classic plays as well as late night productions. During these years Hywel appeared in a number of these shows, the most memorable of which was his performance as the young Laurie Lee in my production of *Cider with Rosie*. Like several other of our productions, it transferred into Town. For this he was nominated in *Variety Magazine* as 'the most promising newcomer to the West End'.

Largely due to the Alexander Technique his stammer had virtually vanished by now. However, during my production of *Letters from an Eastern Front*, in which he had the final long speech, supposedly written by a child who was in Hiroshima when the atom bomb was dropped, he began to suffer from minor hesitations in his speech. Until then he had always acted with others, but here he was on his own and at a climactic moment in the drama. Joyce Bird, his Alexander teacher, came to see a performance and reported back to him that the audience was totally unaware of any hesitation. In spite of this reassurance, however, he began to anguish that his stammer might return and for a while he stopped acting. He began to drift, doing a series of jobs, until one night I went into his bedroom and said, rather dramatically, 'What are you doing with your life?'

This resulted in a long conversation, one of several we were to have during our relationship. At the end of it he declared, 'If I can't act then I will become a teacher of the Alexander Technique.' As a result he took the Teachers Training Course, doing odd jobs to pay for his fees. He became a remarkably gifted teacher of the Technique, whilst continuing to act from time to time. But for his speech impediment, which became so slight that few were even aware of it, he would have had a much more fruitful career both in the theatre and on television as he was naturally photogenic.

In 1969 I launched *Stage Two* as the experimental wing of the Hampstead Theatre. Funds were raised and a company was formed comprising Hywel, Di Trevis,

Paul Sanders, Kevin Costello and Jaarkko Tamminen from Finland. We worked for a whole year in isolation before giving performances of works created entirely by the actors. In 1970, in order to raise money for the new venture, I went on a ten thousand mile lecture tour of America arranged for me by Malcolm Muggeridge via his New York agent, Colston Leigh, while the actors took two weeks out for a holiday before returning to work on their own. Hywel went off to Venice and in his final letter described how he had visited the Peggy Guggenheim Collection of Modern Art which is housed in a low palazzo on the Grand Canal.

> As an ambience the place is marvellous and I sat in the garden a long time. In one corner there are little graves and a plaque on a wall which reads: 'Here lie my babies' – and then a list of the names of about ten dogs such as Pegeen, Madam Butterfly, Peacock, Sir H. And I thought of dear Titus who I still miss.

And then at the end of this letter he added:

> I'm glad we made love before you left for America. I do feel guilty if we go a long time without making love. Sometimes one gets a block which kills desire and it becomes difficult to break, but I think on the whole we solve our difficulties well, and when we do make love it is very good.

Hywel was subject to moods. Sometimes he would withdraw completely, there would be no sexual contact, no emotional response, and once I was so bewildered by his withdrawal that I recall crying out in pain, 'Just hold me! Take me in your arms!' What I was to learn is that in any long relationship there will be these intervals of dryness, of withdrawal. If one truly loves then one accepts these passages, but it takes time.

Hywel used to like going to the *Black Cap* in Camden Town. It was a gay pub and on Saturdays always had a cabaret act where performers such as the celebrated drag artist Mrs Shufflewick appeared. I went once or twice, but, not being at ease in pubs, I was happy for Hywel to go on his own.

One evening he was late back, having said he was having drinks with someone. I knew it was a cover and was aware that earlier he had been out to telephone someone from a kiosk. Also I had come across a note he had written, 'Dear Stanley, I am dying to see you. I shall be on my own the week after next. Love, Hywel.'

When he came in he was clearly excited, his eyes bloodshot. 'I have had an extraordinary evening. I met this cancer doctor – Stanley.' They had been to bed once before, he said, and they had planned to meet that evening, 'And then last night', said Hywel, 'I knew you wanted to go to bed with me, and I didn't because I was meeting with Stanley. Then I had a dream and felt very guilty that I was doing this, so I left a message at his house. I didn't want him to feel I was playing about. But he was in the pub.'

I had been ill at ease for some time, sensing such undercurrents and I found this news deeply disturbing. Yet how to be generous, objective and not magnify the significance of such an incident? 'I find that other sex improves my sex with you,' said Hywel. 'I find sex very exciting. It is important to me.'

I was so inextricably bound up with him that this revelation struck at my very foundations – and yet I knew that I must be more accepting. Somehow I had to try to learn to live with this insecurity. The challenge, it seemed to me, was how to keep afloat and not to be psychologically overwhelmed. I knew I must not isolate this incident but accept that it would almost certainly recur in the years ahead.

I recalled Eleanor Farjeon telling me about a period of two years when she suspected Pod (George Earle, with whom she lived) was having an affair with a nurse, but said nothing. 'I was never very good at sex,' she said, 'and I knew that this was what Pod was getting from this affair, and that it would eventually die out, for we had so much more in common. He was with me to the end. I shall never forget the day he died. Golden Coney, my beloved marmalade cat, sat on the chest of drawers, keeping watch over the bed on which Pod's body lay, and stayed there for three days without moving, not even to eat, until the body was taken away.'

Today, with sexual contacts immediately available online, any long-term relationship or marriage has to learn how to take this on board. It is here that many gay couples have pioneered a form of relationship based on friendship, with various sexual affairs on the side. Such a set-up will not suit everyone, however, for it demands an inner security about the relationship itself, as well as a deep sense of trust in each other.

'The challenge of all committed relationships,' writes Joseph Campbell, 'is to allow the freedom of individual growth within the container of the relationship.' 'Are you trying to possess someone?' he asks, 'or are you in a relationship?' A true and lasting bond requires more than sexual interest and the meeting of mutually unconscious projections. It demands a growing recognition by each partner of the other as a real personality, possessing qualities and expectations over and above those projected. A true love should enable each to fulfil their potential. This is a continuous process of readjustment and discovery. Of course 'the real person' is never discovered at the beginning of a relationship and so there are clashes of temperament; but, if love is to grow, each has to learn how to withdraw his or her psychological projections.

Hywel and I talked it all through, late into the night. Slowly I managed to clear up the pain which my active and jealous imagination had conjured. Gradually we were both able to reach back to our own centre. It is only by facing up to things, by working them through, that the centre is held. Throughout the fifty-four years of our time together we learned to confront several such difficulties and misunderstandings, never seeking to evade them, learning to endure a variety of emotional weathers, discovering that love has many layers – and that it deepens with the years. In the end we became like an old tree that has endured so many storms and whose roots are so deep that nothing can shake it, not even death. And while, at the beginning of our relationship, I was in the role of an elder brother, over the years it was Hywel who taught me so much – so that, in the end, we stood shoulder to shoulder.

Which is why Mario Conti, now a Cardinal, but then Bishop of Aberdeen, was so profoundly wrong when he wrote in *The Tablet* that 'there is an endemic instability in homosexual relationships'. And why the words of Father Timothy Radcliffe, OP, the former Provincial of the Dominican Order in England, are so much wiser:

> Desire, and especially sexual desire, is fundamental to our humanity and our search for God; but often the Church has been afraid of desire and has sought to control it and suppress it, fearful of its power, instead of liberating it for its ultimate aspiration, God. The Church works in terms of a narrow understanding of sex as about producing babies, which is why homosexuality is simply seen as a deviance, and is not recognised as offering a love in which God also may be found.

It is interesting that, as early as 1963, the Society of Friends published *Towards a Quaker View of Sex*, in which it stated:

> Surely it is the nature and quality of a relationship that matters; one must not judge by its outward appearance but by its inner worth. We see no reason why the physical nature of a sexual act should be the criterion by which the question whether or not it is moral should be decided. An act which expresses true affection between two individuals does not seem to us to be sinful by reason alone of the fact that it is homosexual.

∼ 6 ∼

IN 1970 my mother suddenly announced, 'Your father and I are going to live together again.'

'Is that wise?' I asked, remembering their endless bickering and rows, not to mention my father's drinking. 'Oh, we are older now,' answered my mother. 'After all, we are both in our seventies.'

Twenty years previously my father had gone to live and work in America, and my mother to live in Norfolk, but now this news necessitated finding a home for them – a place where Hywel and I could also stay when visiting. It was my mother who discovered The Old Rectory at Bleddfa, a tiny hamlet in Radnorshire, then the least populated county in Britain. Bleddfa had an inn, one telephone kiosk, a small school, and a tiny post-office-cum village shop. Opposite the inn, behind tall trees, was the Old Rectory and, alongside it, the twelfth-century church of St Mary Magdalene. The property was on sale for £6,500 and I had only £2,000 in my savings, but various friends offered to loan the rest. Little did we know how important a part that house and the church were to play in our lives over the years ahead.

My father returned from America. Sadly, in no time at all, the old rows erupted – and the heavy drinking began again. My mother collapsed, some days sleeping for twenty-four hours at a time. I sent for the local doctor who, after inspecting her, pronounced bluntly,

'There is only one thing wrong with your mother, and that is your father!' It was a correct diagnosis. And so I had to break it to my father that he should return to America, a decision he himself had already arrived at. 'It isn't anyone's fault,' I said, 'it is just that you and mother are such totally different people.' And so he went back to the States.

Over the next two years, with remarkable patience, Hywel taught me to drive. Up to then, whenever I was in Wales staying with my mother, I either had to stand in the road and hitch a lift from a passing car or hire a taxi, which I couldn't afford. But I was not an easy pupil and it was a great test of love that Hywel never once lost his cool with me.

One spring day he allowed me to drive as far as Pen-y-Bont Common, where George Fox once converted large numbers of people to Quakerism, many of whom subsequently emigrated to America (which is why in Pennsylvania there are places named after villages in Radnorshire). As one approaches Pen-y-Bont Common the countryside opens up, with mountains in the distance and sheep grazing on the roadside. Ahead we saw an old woman, like a character out of Thomas Hardy, walking along the road towards us, her head and body twisted to one side.

On our return from shopping in Llandrindod Wells, she was still walking and seemed to have made little progress. 'I wonder if she would like a lift?' said Hywel, and so I stopped the car and watched him in the driving mirror as he ran back to speak to her. She came up to the car, but as Hywel went to help her in she winced with pain, snapping 'Let me manage on my own!'

Twisted with arthritis, she lolled in the back seat like a child. She told us that she walked four miles, there and back, each day to Llandrindod to shop. 'It's something to do,' she said. Turning off the main road I drove a mile up a winding steep lane with high banks. 'There's more traffic here than you'd think,' she said. 'Sometimes I have to clamber up the bank to get out of the way.'

'What do you do in winter?' I asked.

'Oh, I've been up to my legs in snow! But this past summer was so hot I had to carry buckets of water up from the farm below.' Then abruptly she said, 'This is it. I'll get out now.'

'This' was a blue-painted wooden house overlooking the valley. Slowly and carefully she slid out of the car, refusing all help, and then, with her head bent to one side, peered up, smiling, to thank us. We helped carry her heavy bags into the bare and decaying house. In the main room where she slept in a chair, there was a strong smell of excrement, crumbs everywhere on the flagstones, and plates of food set down for her two dozen cats, one of which had just peed on the floor. There was an old kitchen range heaped with ashes and an oil stove with a kettle simmering on it.

'What time did you go out?' asked Hywel.

'Eleven,' she replied. It was then three o'clock.

On a chair was a pile of clothes, and on a table unwashed dishes and stale food. She stood, her head bowed, peering at us. 'Soon be Whitsun. It was Whitsun when my husband died. We'd been in to shop, got back, had a cup of tea, and were sitting together when he died. It was such a shock, I couldn't even cry.' As we left, she stood at the door, bidding us be careful as we drove down the lane. 'She's like a bird with one wing,' said Hywel.

Eventually I passed my driving test, but for several months, whenever I was driving from London, Hywel would insist on driving me to Stratford where he would then get on a train back to London, leaving me to drive on to Bleddfa. When I had to return to London I would drive to Stratford where he would get off the train and take over from me for the journey back on the motorway. Only when he was convinced I was up to it did he finally say, 'You are ready now to do the job on your own.'

By 1974 Hywel was established as an Alexander teacher, practising from our flat. With some of his pupils there was so much laughter emanating from his teaching room at the back that I began referring to it as the Laughing Technique! Virginia Brownlow, Molly Keane's youngest daughter, who lived opposite and came almost weekly for her Alexander lesson, wrote after his death:

My Alexander lessons with Hywel meant a great deal to me. He was so welcoming. His teaching room was so simple. At the end of my lesson he used to walk me out onto the balcony, overlooking the tops of trees to the city of London and St Paul's in the distance. I went to him first after I had a bone graft from my hip. The lessons themselves helped me a great deal, but the experience was much more than the lessons. He always had jokes and we both knew that we talked too much! I used to go down the stairs feeling quite different to how I had felt on the way up. Apart from being a few inches taller physically, I used to feel emotionally released and relaxed and smiling. Whenever I met him my spirits lifted.

In addition to his practice as an Alexander teacher, Hywel appeared in a number of my productions over the years, including *The Taming of the Shrew*, with Susan Hampshire and Nicky Henson, *Romeo and Juliet*, *Pericles*, and *Macbeth*. He also worked regularly, for over forty years, at the Royal Opera House as one of the actors used by Peter Hall in ballet and opera.

⪼ 7 ⪻

1975 WAS TO BRING a new drama into our lives. At our New Year's Eve party I met Sean, one of the actors at the Royal Opera House. A few days later I heard Hywel talking to him on the phone and he then came into the room where I was resting. Climbing onto the bed, he did a somersault, and started talking to me, upside down, about Sean. 'Clearly,' I said, 'you are a little head over the heels in love with him!'

We then had one of our long exploratory talks: how being in love is not always connected with sex, and that though love can be painful it can also enlarge one; also that one loves on different levels and my deepest level was with Hywel. 'Sean is special!' said Hywel and so we began to wonder whether it were possible that we three might develop a kind of relationship together that could enrich each one of us, recognising, if it were to be so, that it would call for delicacy and tact, but might also be painful. It was one of those significant clearing-house discussions that we had from time to time.

One evening, over supper and a bottle of wine, Sean spoke about his childhood in County Clare, of families, deaths, drink, illegitimate children and mental homes. He told how he knew from the age of twelve that he was gay, when he met a man in his late twenties with whom he would go for long drives all over Ireland. 'I'd go and sign on at school,' he said, 'then off we would go. I was

49

always playing truant. I was nearly expelled at one point. I never had any problem about being gay. I was always able to accept that that was the way I was. I remember once sitting in front of the fire with my mother when a programme came on the radio about homosexuals. My mother turned it up to listen and I remained hidden behind my newspaper. There was a woman doctor in the studio who claimed she could cure homosexuals. There were about twenty gay men in the studio and they all told her she was wrong. My mother never said anything until it was over – and then she declared, "I'll go and make us a nice cup of tea!"'

The next morning Hywel and I had another talk. He felt we were both becoming too infatuated with Sean and needed to cool it. He also talked about our own relationship, saying, 'I think you underrate it. I don't know of any other couple who still go to bed and make love as we do, after seventeen years. We have grown in all sorts of ways and have continued to explore each other's sexuality.'

Hywel, I learned, had been to bed once with Sean before I met him. Now it was decided that Sean and I should spend a night together in the back room. The next morning I came into the front room to find Hywel seated by the window, sipping a mug of tea. Sensing his desolation I put my arms around him. The tears splashed and suddenly he broke down. I held him close. He had not broken down like this for years. What could be the outcome, I wondered, of a situation in which I was drawn to Sean when, at the same time, there were such deep ties between Hywel and myself. Could the two relationships be contained somehow?

The next day Hywel went down with a temperature of 102 degrees and lay flat out in bed. Days passed. I went to teach his class at the British Drama League and returned to give him lunch. Sitting up perkily in bed he said, 'Until we find somewhere big enough for us three, or you decide to burn your boats and go off with Sean, I have decided to make the front room my teaching room so that you and Sean can have the back room.' He paused and then added, 'I've failed you, haven't I?' I replied that failure did not come into it, but that things change.

'We have been very blessed,' I said. Hywel replied, 'And I brought you Sean: that's part of the pattern too.'

We realised that his unwellness was mainly a reaction to what was happening. Hywel had never experienced jealousy before, but now he did because he felt threatened, and I recalled him telling me how when his sister Mair was born, seven years after his having been Mother's boy, he suddenly felt shut out.

Hywel was now experiencing at close quarters what I had experienced when I returned from my lecture tour of America in 1970. In my absence he had met and befriended Dov, an artist, who had just arrived from Israel and knew no one in London. They had been to bed many times, been together to concerts, and he had been introduced to our mutual friends, so that when, on my return, I met him for the first time, seated at our dinner table, clearly at home in our flat, I suffered the most intense jealousy as I realised how much they had shared during my absence. It felt as though I had died and that he had taken my place, even sleeping in my bed. And yet, and yet, I knew that even this was good, to have the egg (ego) cracked in order to release new growth. (Eventually Dov went to live and work in Amsterdam where he found his life partner.)

In the midst of the situation with Sean, I was whisked away to South Africa to direct a production of Tennessee Williams' *A Streetcar Named Desire.* On my return I experienced a strong reunion with Hywel – but Sean? He said he would telephone but didn't. I was puzzled as we had been apart for five weeks. Why was he being evasive?

In the meantime Hywel had had two significant dreams. In the first he dreamed of a house on Parliament Hill which was owned by me. Neither of us lived there for it was over-run by squatters and rapidly deteriorating. Yet, because the house was furnished, they could by law be turned out. This dream seemed to indicate that our situation was not without hope. In the second dream Hywel was trying to get into the back room of our flat and found he couldn't. When he finally did, it was all changed. He found that I had built a much larger balcony which the builder had left unfinished and was, therefore, dangerous, while a large part of the roof was exposed to the sky.

His dreams made me realise that I was the real threat to our relationship and that in becoming so emotionally involved with Sean it was I who had led us into this quagmire. And yet I did not know how to resolve it.

In the end it was Sean who took the initiative and

broke off the relationship with Hywel and myself, his deepest instinct telling him it would not work. There was an important lesson to be learned from this: that in any long-term relationship there is the inevitability that one or the other, or both, may be attracted to a third person. And yet, the only religious group I know of that has addressed this issue is the Society of Friends. To quote once again from *Towards a Quaker View of Sex*:

The sexual drive differs in strength and frequency in different individuals, and what is customary and normal in one marriage may not be in another. Similarly it may differ as between the partners of a marriage, and from time within each of them. In all such differences great patience, sympathy, and encouragement born of love are required to overcome many disharmonies, both temporary and of long duration. This is probably the point at which to mention the so-called triangular situation. This is too often thought of as a wholly destructive and irresponsible relationship, the third party being at least an intruder and at worst an unscrupulous thief. Its portrayal thus in fiction and drama no doubt contributes to the stereotype. But it would be regarded as dull indeed to describe the happy and instructive resolution of such a situation. Not sufficient recognition is given to the fact that a triangular situation can and often does arise in which all three persons behave responsibly, are deeply conscious of the difficulties, and equally anxious to avoid injury to the others.

I shall never forget, at the height of the situation, when we were staying with my mother in Bleddfa, Hywel saying, 'You are more to me than I am to myself. I want you to be happy. I won't make any difficulties. You have been a very stabilising influence in my life. I can't imagine living with anyone else. I've never met anyone else I wanted to live with, not that I have been looking at people with this thought. I am rarely jealous, but I was jealous when we were in a restaurant once and you said, "I've danced with that waiter." And then I thought, but I live with him!'

We wandered down a dark lane together, deep in the Welsh countryside, an owl screeching like an old bike tyre being pumped up. Then we climbed to the top of the nearby hill. Immediately below us was a field of shorn sheep, silent in the moonlight. We gently embraced as we resolved our problems.

Ours was a relationship that continued to grow, bringing forth new leaf and shedding the old. One day, after we had made love in the back room (always Hywel referred to it as making love, not just having sex), the sun pouring in, and music surrounding us like the sea, the thought came to me that if one goes far enough into the forest one comes to a place of rest. After twenty years our love-making was deep and strong and controlled, fashioned from years of insight into each other's body, yearnings and experience. And always Hywel's deep passionate cry: 'Oh, my darling, I love you, I love you, I love! We love each other don't we?'

Listening recently to an impassioned performance by the Busch Ensemble of Brahms' *Piano Quartet in G*

Minor, Opus 25, I turned to my companion and likened it to the most perfect love-making. 'But,' he replied, 'there is so much pain and anguish in it!' To me, however, the act of making love, at its highest, involves the whole of one's being and all of our longing to be one with the beloved. It is that which drives us towards a climax of total union which we also know in advance is temporary, though after the ecstasy there is the calm as of a sea after a storm when the waves gently ripple.

I think of a line from the poet St John Perse: 'So little time to be born to this instant. The cry of the god is upon us.' But it is only honest to say that sex without love can also be very releasing, simply on a natural level. Of course it can also become a drug when the physical need becomes insatiable and life turns into a series of one night stands. But if the rare heights of love-making are the summit, it has to be acknowledged that among the lower hills of sex there is much delight also to be found. None of us can be judgmental.

~ 8 ~

ONE MORNING I was woken at 8 a.m. by the sound of the telephone. I heard Hywel answering it. He called out to me. It was his brother-in-law, Jac, ringing to say that Catherine, Hywel's mother, had died that night. I lay with Hywel, holding him in silence, reflecting how curious it was that both our mothers were named Catherine.

I wrote to my friend, Sister Meinrad Craighead, at Stanbrook Abbey, to ask her prayers for Hywel and his mother. Then, a few days later, Hywel drove off for the funeral in Llangynog. On his return he wrote to thank Sister Meinrad:

> Thank you so much for your thoughts and prayers during my mother's illness and now her sudden death. Your lovely card was here when I returned from Wales. I was shattered by the funeral which took place in the chapel where my mother took me by the hand as a little boy, and the memory of this early relationship flared up with great force. Also the pain in my mother's life – she had had a lot of mental illness following the birth of my youngest sister. I cried for her pain as she lay under the flowers, free from it all. I think you are right – I shall be closer to her now and her memory will remain green until I die. We are fortunately a close family and of great support to each other. I hope very much that you will find your way to calmer waters. [Meinrad, too, had recently lost her mother]. With much, much gratitude, Hywel.

~ 9 ~

We are in Wales and I wake to the sound of a whistle and a voice calling, 'Jimmie!' It is five o'clock in the morning. I look out of my bedroom window and see Hywel below in the garden, in jeans and a red check shirt. 'Come for a walk!' he says. Although woken from a deep sleep, I get dressed and go down to join him. There is a white mist everywhere. At the farm, geese waddle noisily away, while three horses and a foal loom up out of the mist to stare at us.

Everywhere there is this hushed silence, no birds singing as yet. Everything is focused by the mist. When we return, an hour later, the mist is rising and the sense of secrecy has gone. It is now six o'clock and it has become an everyday world.

Hywel comes into my bedroom in Wales, draws back the curtains and says, 'See what's outside!' It is snowing. The flakes, trembling, leaping, zig-zagging like children let out of school, come tumbling down with such a silent abandon of release. Everything is hushed. The white summer house at the bottom of the garden, which is seventy years old, looks whiter still, while the panes of glass reflect the trees with their dusting of snow.

The anniversary of our first meeting and the tenderness and vitality of the relationship constantly moves me: that we frequently stop, when moving about the flat, to embrace and kiss, responding to each other like ships sailing familiar straits, knowing also the deep waters and the dangerous rocks, respecting the limits.

Since his mother's death, sometimes in the morning I come down from my loft and lie for a while with Hywel. He drinks at my lips – a deep, contented, baby-like imbibing. He often implies, as he said again today and has in the past, that he will die first.

[*How strange and moving it is to realise now how accurately he intuited his own end.*]

I have a dream in which Hywel and I are to perform an improvised dance. A white sheet is unrolled as the music starts, and Hywel and I move onto it to begin. Melody and movement fuse, with Hywel at the very centre of the dance. We flow across the sheet, leaping, turning, flying. It is our life being danced: its togetherness, and our awareness of one another.

Reflecting on this dream I recall the old carol:

Tomorrow shall be my dancing day
I would my true love did so dance
To see the legend of my play,
To call my true love to the dance.
Sing, oh! Love, oh! My Love! My love. My Love.
This have I done for thee my true love.

[*I have had these words calligraphed on white canvas by John Rowlands Pritchard, and they hang on a wall as a reminder of all that we shared.*]

Evening. We are seated in the deepening dusk, sheltered against the rain in the swing hammock under the arbour with its perspex roof, and the lights inside the Old Rectory making it look like a welcoming lantern. Tired after working long hours in the garden, but content, Hywel talks about spirituality, attempting to define it as that which is unworldly, non-material, affording a glimpse of the infinite and unchanging.

Hywel gives me an Alexander lesson – 'Be focused but not intense' – as the snow drifts slowly down, feathering the trees and forming caps on the potted plants and the flowering winter jasmine on our rooftop balcony, so that it looks like a Zen courtyard above the tops of the trees. There is a feeling of warmth and peace. At the end of the lesson Hywel turns me towards the window and makes me bow down in homage to the snow, then reach high with my arms outstretched like the branches of the trees receiving the snow.

When watching television Hywel sits on his haunches within three feet of the set, in total concentration, like a child, his forehead puckered, while one hand tugs at his toenails. Each moment of drama, tension, pain or comedy is mirrored in his face. Often he looks across to me to share what is happening.

When having a bath, which is very much a morning ritual for him, Hywel can be heard snorting like a hippopotamus. Rising from the water to dry himself, he stands there, eyes bright and humorous, then stoops towards me as I enter and our lips meet and melt.

One evening Hywel says quietly, thoughtfully, 'We may have lost our innocence but that other evening of lovemaking seemed to me very close to a state of innocence: our loving was so deep, aware, tender, grave and gentle.'

I am woken in my loft bedroom by two orange balloons floating up, inscribed 'I love you'. Then a third balloon appears and with it Hywel's smiling face as he brings up his birthday gifts for me.

Hywel in *Deaths and Entrances*, created by Stage Two in 1970

James in the rain!

Hywel on his bed with Titus

Hywel's ritual morning bath

James, Hywel and dog on a Radnorshire hillside

Hywel with James's mother

Hywel with Kathleen Raine at Bleddfa

Hywel in the back garden at the Old Rectory

James and Hywel in Ireland

Hywel creating the garden at Ballywilliam

Hywel reading of an evening

James in the same room looking up to smile at Hywel

Hywel coming into Waterloo Lodge from the woods

∾ *10* ∾

I T WAS in 1973 that the Rector of Bleddfa Church came to tell me that the twelfth-century church of St Mary Magdalene was on a provisional list for closure. All over the country at that time churches were being declared redundant at the rate of two a week, and in Radnorshire there were some that were even razed to the ground.

What could be done to prevent this? Having founded the Hampstead Theatre on a shoestring and for seven years, without any grants, lurching from one financial crisis to another, I was not eager to save a small church in a tiny hamlet in the least populated county in Britain.

Over the following months Hywel and I discussed this, and came to the reluctant conclusion that if we did nothing no one else would. Launching the Hampstead Theatre had been an act of faith and whatever was done for Bleddfa Church would be the same. I suggested to the Rector that if we waited until a redundancy order was slapped on the church it would be too late to protest. If the church were to be saved we had to act now.

In Paul Roberston's recent book *Soundscapes* there is a fascinating quotation:

Until one is committed, there is hesitancy, the chance to draw back, always ineffectiveness. Concerning all acts of initiative and creation there is one elementary truth, the ignorance of which kills countless ideas and splendid plans: that the moment one definitely commits one's self, then providence moves too. A whole stream of events issues from the decision, raising in one's favour all manner of unforeseen incidents, meetings and material assistance, which no man could have dreamt would have come his way.

This was abundantly true in what came to pass in Bleddfa. Since the church was still in use for worship – albeit with only one service a week and an average congregation of four – I suggested that, while continuing to be used for worship, it could be developed as a Centre for Sacred Art, offering a programme of exhibitions, seminars, retreats, concerts and workshops. The Rector responded warmly to this and it was put to the parish council and passed. In this way the Bleddfa Church Restoration Society was formed. I then wrote to George Pace, the leading church architect at that time, who generously donated his services, drawing up a scheme for re-ordering the church so that it could be used in a variety of ways. This was then submitted to the Diocese for what is called a Faculty, giving permission for the work to go ahead.

Through the sculptor Simon Verity, we contacted Roger Capps of Capps and Capps in Hay-on-Wye, a firm that specialised in restoring old buildings, and invited them to come and inspect the building. He discovered that not only did one major beam and two new sets of trusses need replacing: the entire roof needed to be overhauled – the wooden pegs which held the existing tiles in place, had all rotted, so that the tiles were held together solely by gravity! The roof therefore had to be stripped, re-battened, re-felted, and new tiles installed, each with a steel pin. In addition the building needed complete re-wiring. Then, when the Victorian pews were removed, the bare earth on which they stood had to be flag-stoned.

In the autumn of 1974 an appeal was launched. Hywel and I organised a concert in the church to announce the scheme, declaring that although we were few in number, we had only to reach out our hands and others would come to join us in an ever-growing circle. It was in this way that the Bleddfa Centre for Caring and the Arts (later to be renamed the Bleddfa Centre for the Creative Spirit) was born, based on my belief that the arts should nurture and enrich people's lives. In 1978 we were registered as a charity under the name of The Bleddfa Trust, with the aim of 'providing a centre for those seeking through prayer, through the arts, and through encounter with others, a deepening of spiritual understanding'.

I was convinced that we had to re-think the meaning of 'community' in connection with rural areas. It was apparent that in many parts of the country the old unity of a village or hamlet was already a thing of the past. The increasing closure of village schools and sub-post offices, the dwindling congregations at churches and chapels – the incumbent often having to minister to some eight or ten churches – plus the drift of younger people to towns and urbanised areas where there was a greater chance of employment, not to mention the gradual disappearance of the small-holding farmer, like Hywel's father, had had the effect of debilitating many rural areas. If a village, especially a small one, were to survive into the twenty-first century, it would have to redefine the meaning of the word 'community'. Each would be forced to find its own solution in a pragmatic fashion based on local conditions and local resources.

Once the pews had been removed, Hywel and I drove to Sussex, to a church that wanted to get rid of its chairs, and was happy to let us have them for free. The chairs were stored in our barn at the Old Rectory. Each time there was an event Hywel and I would carry them, two on each arm, to set up for a workshop or a concert, and then afterwards carry them back to the barn, so that the church would be ready for the following morning's service. Over time, regular visitors to the concerts would help us carry the chairs back to our barn.

The first three years saw a programme of workshops, retreats, events for children, and exhibitions of art (mounted by Hywel) by such outstanding artists as Thetis Blacker and Peter Eugene Ball. The poet Kathleen Raine came to speak, and there were concerts by the Claydon Ensemble, Leon Goossens, Osian Ellis, and The York Winds of Toronto, all giving their services free. Throughout all this, Hywel and I acted as hosts, having many of the artists and performers to stay at the Old Rectory.

I wrote countless letters, and it was in response to one that Lord Anglesey, then Chairman of the Historic Buildings Trust, secured us a major grant of £50,000 towards the work of restoration. A substantial sum, but still only half the amount needed – so more letters had to be written!

At Easter and Christmas the Church congregation would swell to six or seven, and it was Hywel who one day suggested that if there were a simple service of carols and readings on Christmas Eve, separate from the regular Communion service on Christmas Day, the church would be packed. Christmas Eve, he argued, is 'a threshold time when many people feel utterly lonely, their children having grown up and left home, or partners having died'. The Rector initially opposed this suggestion, but I persisted until he said, 'Oh, alright! Provided you organise it and I just give a blessing at the end!'

The Rector arrived on Christmas Eve to find the church packed. Instead of the usual set-up, with rows of chairs facing the altar, they had been arranged in a circle, four chairs deep, around a manger filled with straw. The raftered roof was softly illuminated but otherwise there was darkness: a warm, hushed atmosphere as everyone sat pondering the words, 'The people who sat in darkness have seen a great light.' Then, at a given signal, from outside on the green, the children from the village school, wrapped and muffled against the cold, could be heard raucously singing a *Gloria* as they advanced up the path to the church, with a boisterous ringing of handbells, gourds, tambourines and drums. Inside, everyone waited while in the porch there was a hushed consultation and whispers of 'Go on, Robert!'

Little Robert Gittoes then gave three loud bangs on the door of the church.

'Who is it?' I called.

'It is the Christ Child,' replied young Robert.

To which I responded, 'Let the Christ Child enter!'

The doors opened and the children came inside, two by two, carrying tall candles, farm lanterns and baskets of mince pies. Finally, there appeared a brother and sister bearing a life-size figure of a naked newborn baby which they placed in the manger. Candles were lit and passed round, and then, very softly, all joined in singing 'Away in a Manger'. The faces of young and old, church and chapel, believers and non-believers, friends and visitors, were reflected in the light from the flickering candles. There was music from melodion, cello and flute. Carols were sung, a poem was read by one of the children, followed by a short meditation and prayers which I led, then more carols. The mince pies were blessed and then people began to move quietly about, eating mince pies and drinking coffee, something unheard of in church at that time, talking in small groups, not wanting to leave, simply content to be there in the candlelight, in the warmth and security of that ancient house of prayer. It was as though, on that dark winter's eve, they had finally come to a safe place.

Because of dwindling numbers the tiny village school was eventually closed by Powys County Council, and with its closure the hamlet began to die. No longer did mothers assemble to collect their children at the end of the day or call in at the village shop (in time both the shop and sub-post office were closed down too). So it became important to try and preserve the school-house as a public building. More letters were written and money was raised to buy it for the Bleddfa Trust, to provide a gallery, offices and a tearoom, as well as a garden. It became the official centre for the Trust and was formally opened by the Marchioness of Anglesey in 1983. Some time later, three dilapidated barns and a plot of land adjoining the old school came on the market. These, too, were acquired by the Trust, helped considerably by a grant from the Foundation for Sport and the Arts; and the buildings were converted into the handsome Barn Centre where regular workshops are now run.

Over the years many lives have been enriched by these workshops for, in the words of Bleddfa's chief patron, Rowan Williams, then Archbishop of Canterbury:

> It is by encouraging the creative spirit in everyone that we help them to become fully human. Bleddfa is a place where people, ideas and imagining meet at a depth, in a way that is rare. I think it represents all that is most hopeful for our anxious and fragmented culture.

Throughout the first twenty-five years of the Bleddfa Centre, Hywel played a crucial role as co-founder. Just as he transformed the church for the Christmas Eve service, so his strong sense of the visual enabled him to transform it for major exhibitions. Of the work of the Trust he was to write, 'To share with others has always been central to the vision of Bleddfa. The work of the Bleddfa Trust deepens the quality of life, living as we do in an excessively materialistic age. Bleddfa is seeking to keep this materialism at bay. It stands for nourishment and healing, for the inner life of people. It is a place for celebration.'

∾ 11 ∾

IN JULY 1983 Hywel and I flew to Grand Rapids in Michigan. I was to teach a course on ritual for an Experimental Theatre Summer School there, and Hywel was to teach the Alexander Technique. On arrival we were taken to our accommodation, a small house on the edge of a ravine. The humidity was overwhelming and there was no air-conditioning. In the night a storm erupted with sheet and fork lightning, followed by a tumultuous downpour of rain.

The next morning, at about eleven, the sky turned a dark grey, all light receding, so that inside the house it was like dusk. Doors banged in the wind, trees shaking vigorously, dead leaves leaping, thrown several feet in the air. Then it grew even darker as the first drops of rain spattered down. Leaves skidded past or were hurled along, like hordes fleeing from an advancing army. Thunder rumbled. The wind was now so savage that green leaves were ripped from twigs and sent hurtling downwards, while the trunks of trees swayed, their branches bent backwards, like someone's arm being twisted. Lightning cracked the face of the sky with crinkled lines. The next day we heard on the news of many deaths from heat in places such as Arkansas.

Hywel spent some of the time in Michigan absorbed in reading Laurens van der Post's biography of Carl Jung, whom he regarded as 'the most spiritual man I know of'. Hywel seemed so serene and patient and content to be there. More and more I found myself learning from him. His was a true Zen-like quality of being in the present moment. Word had also got around about what a fine teacher he was of the Alexander Technique, with the result that he had a long list of students wanting to have sessions with him.

Finally, the course was completed and we flew to Toronto to be met by our friend Lex Dashnaw and his partner Douglas. Together they drove us through New Hampshire and Vermont. We then took the ferry over Lake Champain until we arrived at their farm. There we were greeted by George. George, a concert pianist, and Lex, a conductor, had been a couple, until Lex had met Douglas, also a musician, and for decades the three of them had shared their lives together.

In the evenings, while George cooked dinner, Hywel and I shared a sauna with Lex and Douglas and then ran out, under a full moon, to dive into the nearby lake, with the stars glittering overhead and mist swirling on the mountain top.

One day while we were there, some workmen arrived with bulldozers to clear vegetation around their farm-house, revealing, in the process, three enormous upright rocks, clustered together, like guardians of the place. I dreamed of creating a ritual for our friends in which they would stand, hands linked, by the three stones, while they repeated the words, 'May this circle never be broken.' For it seemed to me that the society of three they had created, whatever stresses it might have caused from time to time, such as Hywel and I had experienced with Sean, seemed to contain such richness of sharing within it.

∾ *12* ∾

I REMEMBER THE night so well: it was May 1988 and I had been with my friend the theatre agent, Penny Wesson, to see Michael Gambon in *Uncle Vanya*. On my return I found Hywel seated at my desk, increasingly a favourite place of his when I was not there. A record was playing quietly in the background. We talked about the play and then, in a pause, he said, 'I have spoken with Roel in Amsterdam and I am afraid the news is serious. And it might affect us both. He has AIDS.'

Roel was a gentle soul Hywel had met on a visit to Amsterdam. Hywel had only had sex with him once but felt he could be infected and that he, too, might be HIV Positive. As he talked his eyes glowed and his whole being was totally present, but there was also fear – I could actually smell it. I knelt and held him in my arms and we stayed very close. We talked quietly and gently and then retired to bed. I lay on my bed in the little attic above where Hywel slept, confronting this fear, this darkness of mortality.

To have AIDS at that time was, in effect, a death sentence. In 1987 between five and ten million people worldwide, both gay and straight, were living with the disease. By 1999 this figure had risen to thirty-three million and it was estimated that some fourteen million had already died of it. Today, thanks to advances in medication, it is no longer such a death sentence, and there is much more awareness of the importance of using condoms when having sex. Still, some 1.1 million people die of AIDS every year, and according to the Elton John Foundation, nineteen million of the thirty-five million people living with AIDS worldwide do not even know they have the virus. At the time of its outbreak, with no possible cure in sight, it represented a dire threat to both gay and straight people.

Hywel had developed a temperature, and there were signs of inflammation in his groin. Two days later he wrote to Dennis Barratt, a healer in Bristol, who had been recommended to us by Oliver Caldecott, my editor at Rider Books. At the same time he also made an appointment for an acupuncture session with Alethea Crichton in order to build up his immune system.

The next day Hywel felt better; the temperature and the inflammation had gone. He was quickly back to his cheerful self. But when I returned from teaching he was once more in a state of fear, his groin having flared up again. 'I'm so sorry!' he said and then broke down. I repeated that deep inside I was confident he was not even HIV Positive and that it was fear doing this to him, else why did the symptoms appear so suddenly on learning about Roel? 'Whatever happens,' he declared, 'this is a crossroads for me.'

'Whether you are HIV Positive or not, that is true,' I said. 'Our task is to support each other. But you do need to confront these fears.' I suggested he take the HIV test but he was too afraid to do that.

The healer, Dennis Barratt, replied to Hywel, saying he

was already applying absent healing each night at 11 p.m. It was arranged that Hywel and I would drive to Bristol the following week to see him. Hywel was immediately comforted by talking with him. That evening, at eleven, seated in the front room, Hywel went into a very deep meditation, keeping vigil with Dennis Barratt, while upstairs in my attic bedroom I said a rosary. During the night, as I lay awake, I could almost sense Hywel's fear rising up through the floorboards from below. Then I heard his voice: 'Are you awake?' I climbed down my ladder and lay beside him, and we entered into a state of deep breathing, quietude and near sleep. I was deeply conscious of a presence surrounding him, holding him, embracing both of us. Then I heard an inner voice saying very strongly, very clearly, 'The Mothers are here'. And with this I knew then that all was well, and after half an hour I went back up to my bed, leaving Hywel fast asleep.

There is no doubt in my mind that the word was 'Mothers' and not 'Mother'. Years later, when discussing this episode, our friend the Jungian analyst Dr Anthony Stevens observed, 'The mother who each of us carries in our psyche is a combination of the archetypal Mother and the personal mother who nurtures us. She is a complex made up of those aspects of the Mother archetype that the personal mother succeeds in evoking in the child's maturing psyche. I think "the Mothers" who succoured you and Hywel at that important moment were the positive aspects of the mother complex in both your psyches.'

The next morning Hywel went to the acupuncturist Alethea Crichton for treatment and he told her everything, including a worry that his feet felt very cold. She replied that he was clearly still reeling from the initial shock and resultant fear (to have cold feet was a sign of being frightened). I remained confident that he was in the clear.

The next week I drove Hywel to Bristol to see Dennis Barratt. They had almost an hour together while I walked in the nearby park, saying the rosary, deeply confident that Hywel was okay. When he emerged he told me that Dennis Barratt had already consulted his spiritual guide 'who says I am absolutely in the clear. He has also given me a reflexology exercise for my lymph gland. In addition he also said, "If you don't believe me you can always take an HIV test."'

I drove Hywel to the station to catch a train back to London while I went on to Wales. But when I spoke to him the next day on the telephone, I could sense he was very low, having hardly slept at all and woken up with cold feet once more. He was frightened that he could not sleep. 'Can you articulate what it is you fear?' I asked, and he replied, 'One of the forms of AIDS is that it affects the brain ...' and then he broke down into sobs. I repeated that he did not know whether he was even HIV Positive, let alone suffering from AIDS. I drove back to London at once.

'It is such a comfort, you being here,' he said. He was low and vulnerable but agreed with me that, like his mother, he had a tendency to brood and be negative. Two days later he was still unable to sleep – so again I climbed down and lay with him till dawn.

The following morning he said, 'Feel my brow. And I have only been washing the floor tiles!' Once again he was in a state. It was, I realised, because of this deep fear that we were not yet out of the woods.

Alethea Crichton reported that his fire and water 'elements' were not flowing, hence the heat going to his head and the cold to his feet. She said he might have to take the blood test so that he would know one way or another rather than continue in this limbo of uncertainty, but he was still frightened of doing this. Alethea asks him, 'Deep down inside, tell me spontaneously, without stopping to think, is there anything you wish for yourself?' to which Hywel replied, 'There is nothing I could wish for myself since I have known such incredible good fortune. It is only for others I wish I could do something.'

I left a message for the nuns of Stanbrook Abbey, asking them to pray that he might be delivered from this darkness of fear, and be filled instead with light and grace and strength. Then I drove down to Wales on my own and for the first time found myself infected with fear. On Thursday morning I visited my priest friend John Hencher. As soon as I arrived, he asked, 'How's Hywel?' I replied, 'He's fine.' John then said, 'It's an AIDS scare, isn't it?'

'How on earth did you know?' I asked. 'I haven't spoken to anyone about it.'

'I just knew,' he said. 'And he's clear!' The next day, while knowing that he had certain psychic gifts, I asked him how he knew. 'I just knew,' he replied. 'Like I always know when it is you telephoning.'

I told Hywel all this when I telephoned and he was comforted. 'I trust John,' he said.

At the Old Rectory I stayed in bed sleeping until half past three in the afternoon, drained and exhausted.

Hywel was in danger of losing his confidence and his wonderful affirmative spirit. He wept often – though in some ways that was good. And once, when driving the car, he broke down and I had to take over. One day he asked me to lead him in a visualisation. As we sat in silence, he began to describe what he saw: He had descended into a stone temple where he had found a small stone, something that was of great value …

Afterwards he said the pain was that he might die unfulfilled. Later, when giving me an Alexander lesson, he said how he felt our love had deepened all the more through this crisis.

Later that day he went off to buy some Bach flower remedies. Clearly he was torturing himself, swinging from one mood to another, examining his body for every sign, assuming it to be a symptom of something worse. One night, after a meditation, supper and rest, as I walked him to his friends Owen and Marjorie Richmond, he asked, 'Shall I tell them? Someone will have to, if I am HIV Positive. Will you?' and I replied, 'You are jumping several guns! You don't even know if you are HIV Positive, and even if you were, it doesn't follow that you'll get AIDS!'

One morning I looked up from my desk and saw Hywel's face breaking apart, tears flooding as he sobbed, 'It's the regret at what I have done,' he cried. 'Why? Why did I do it?'

He then took some of the Bach Rescue Remedy and at once became calmer. Dear God, I prayed, let him be clear. I still believed he was.

A few days later, after a shared meditation, he said he was beginning to learn that he must transcend his feelings and allow his mind to be detached, because to yield to his feelings was to give in to negativity, to be blown hither and thither from one moment to the next. Before our shared meditation that day Hywel spoke of feeling 'cast out from Eden'. We talked about the importance of sexuality to him. He referred to himself as 'a pleasure-loving baby'. Sex went very deep for him – it was not that he was promiscuous but it had for him a strong spiritual and maternal quality about it. Yet he also recognised that it was time for the baby to grow up!

I read to him a passage from a book about the importance of affirmations. We then sat cross-legged on the floor and meditated. Afterwards he said, 'I ought to write down my affirmations. They are like mantras.' So I gave him a small book in which to write them down and he also wrote them out on a card so that he could carry that with him.

Here are his affirmations:

> I will be whole again
> I will be healed
> For Jimmie and all the people I love
> And who love me
> I will have courage and be strong
> I will heal myself

I will find joy and peace again
I am getting better all the time

The following morning Hywel said, 'I'm sinking back a bit: I keep having regrets. Why did I do it?' He took some more of the Bach Rescue Remedy and then went off to rehearsal at the Royal Opera House. I stood on our balcony watching him walk down Belsize Grove. Suddenly, as though he sensed me there, he turned to look back. I raised my arm and waved. He walked on but twice more he looked back and I was still there, and again I raised my arm.

After our shared meditations we had made it a practice to raise our arms in a gesture of affirmation. I was reminded of an improvisation he once did at Stage Two when, suddenly and urgently, he drew down from above an imaginary rope, pulling it into himself and, in the process, becoming calmer and stronger. It was on this inner strength deep within him that he now needed to draw.

Finally, one afternoon, he was resolved. Together we walked to the Royal Free Hospital to have a blood test.

The next morning, about 7:30, he appeared through my trapdoor. 'Will you come down?' he asked. He had had a terrible night, full of regrets. I held him in my arms and suggested he make his affirmations. I heard him quietly murmuring, 'Oh, God, forgive me, forgive me!' I placed a hand on his head and blessed him. Then I dragged out cushions and made up a bed for him on the verandah, and got him to lie there, above the treetops, beneath a cloudless sky, while I prepared breakfast.

In the afternoon he had another session with Alethea and then went off to the Opera House for a dress rehearsal with masks and helmets. He was frightened of the heat but we did a meditation before he left. At 6:30 I said a rosary for him very carefully, remembering Jesus' agony in the garden when he sweated with fear, then the crowning with thorns, a symbol of mental torture and suffering. At 8:30 Hywel telephoned to say it had gone well and they were finishing early, so I drove in to collect him. Apparently he had had a very good session with Alethea, as a result of which he went calmly through the rehearsal. The next day he went through the whole of the dress rehearsal without any problems.

The following Wednesday we did a meditation together and then I went with him to the Royal Free Hospital for the result of his blood test. I sat downstairs, meditating. Suddenly I heard his voice, 'Jimmie! It's alright!' and his eyes filled with tears. He was absolutely clear, as both Dennis Barratt and John Hencher had told him. We celebrated by having coffee and croissants, and I telephoned Stanbrook Abbey with the good news and arranged for flowers to be sent for the Lady Chapel.

'I feel as though I have been born again!' laughed Hywel. After months of anxiety it was indeed a blessing. It took a few days for his body to re-adjust before he began to look his usual glowing self.

Then he was off with the Royal Opera House, as one of the actors, to Korea and Japan, visiting Osaka and its famous Zen gardens. On his arrival he received a letter from me telling him of the death of his brother Emyr and that I would attend the funeral on his behalf. Hywel wrote back:

How sad about Emyr, with his uneven and unhappy life, and though our relationship was non-existent, I found the news of his death very disturbing. Masses of small memories came bubbling to the surface. He was only three years older than me, but somehow he was at the end of the line and his health had given way. I remember his huge physical strength working on the farm when he was young, much stronger than me.

And so I drove to Llangynog. The sky was clear with amethyst clouds, the countryside a rich green after all the rains. I arrived early and was shown into the chapel, to a pew behind the family. In front was the preacher's high desk with a squared off section for the chapel elders. The coffin stood to one side with three wreaths on top, including the one I had brought on behalf of Hywel. Slowly the chapel filled up and there was a quiet murmuring of voices like bees in a hive. Then the family entered and we all rose. A young preacher in a three-piece suit spoke in Welsh, every now and then using English words and phrases such as 'we come not to stay but go' and 'out of prison into a palace'. We sang Welsh hymns with melodies of such poignancy that, although I did not understand the words, I sensed their articulation of a longing to be with Christ. An elder then led us in prayer and after a final hymn we filed out into the graveyard. The valley was strangely silent, not even the usual bleating of sheep. A river of people, all dressed in black, flowed out of the chapel to gather round the grave with its imitation grass drapes down the sides.

Emyr's grave was just below that of his parents, by a hedge where apples were ripening on a tree and elderberries clustering. In the background the mountains rose steeply on either side of the valley. After the coffin was lowered, the family went to take one last look. Their grief was so open that I decided I should quietly withdraw and drive off, but I couldn't because so many cars were blocking the way. Then I heard a voice calling 'Jimmie!' and it was Jac, Hywel's sister Heulwen's husband, who urged me to join the family for the funeral tea which was laid out on a long trestle table in a narrow room at the back of the chapel.

The walls were hung with framed photographs of former chapel elders, and the table loaded with bread and butter, Welsh cakes, scones, jellies and plates of ham. Gathered round the table were the generations of Hywel's family, including Aunt Sally stooping on her crutches. I helped to serve food. There was much quiet talk and reminiscence of Emyr, and I found the whole experience very healing. Hywel's good fortune, and that of his sisters, was to have been born and brought up in such a close-knit, supportive community, one where everyone would help with the hay-making or herding the sheep for shearing or dipping, or gathering stones before ploughing a field. Such a close-knit community could, of course, become claustrophobic, which is in part why so many young people left Wales, emigrating to the big cities, just as Hywel did, and so too his sister Mair. Yet for Hywel,

as for Mair, his annual visits were like pilgrimages, emotionally deeply important, while that early influence of
being part of a larger family was reflected in the way he
did so many small tasks for others, such as shopping for
an old lady, or giving someone a lift to the hospital or to
church: countless small acts of kindness to other people.

∼ 13 ∼

IT WAS in October 1988 that Hywel and I were staying with Molly Keane in Ardmore, County Waterford.
Seated in the dusk before a fire of logs and peat, with
Hero, her dachshund, asleep on her lap – having been
given scraps of buttered scone – Molly began to tell us
about the time, some forty years earlier, when she was not
only a successful novelist, writing under the pseudonym
of M.J. Farrell, but was also the toast of London theatre,
having written four plays with her hunting friend, John
Perry, each of which had been directed by John Gielgud
and produced in the West End by Binkie Beaumont,
then the most powerful impresario in London. Her first
play, *Spring Meeting*, was a portrait of John Perry's father,
played by Roger Livesey. 'Everyone came from Ireland
for the first night and it was a huge success. It was at the
Ambassadors Theatre where you had your production
of *84 Charing Cross Road*. But then Bobby, my husband,
died – that was in 1938 – and I stopped writing.'

It was through Hywel that I had got to know Molly
Keane. For many years he taught the Alexander Technique
to her youngest daughter, Virginia Brownlow, who lived
opposite us. When, after a gap of forty years, at the age
of seventy-seven, Molly published her *tour de force*, *Good
Behaviour*, she came frequently to London for television
and press interviews. On one of these visits we loaned
her our flat for a week while we were away in Wales.

I had suggested she might write a play about old age, since she was living through it. I felt sure there was a black comedy there waiting to be written. Once Hero had retreated to his basket Molly got out the notes she had been making. Hywel and I sat entranced as she unfolded what she described as 'the shadow of an idea only'. Based on a true story, it was to be about an elderly woman living in a large house on an island in the West of Ireland. The mistress of the house has just taken on a new companion whom she does not like: 'Two old ladies, one older, one younger, playing their memories against each other, the power of the past over the present.' Once a week the Church of Ireland parson rows over to offer Holy Communion. When the parson arrives he asks the mistress of the house, 'Would your companion like Holy Communion?' to which she replies, 'Oh, she'll eat anything!' – a pure Molly Keane line!

As she sprawled in her chair, playing with her spectacles, I thought what a richness of life she had known, fearless in youth as well as old age, and yet objective about herself. I reminded her of the words of Henry James: 'Observe the oncome of old age. Observe greed. Observe my own despondency. By that means it becomes serviceable.' And Molly recalled how, recently, alone in the kitchen one night, she looked out of the window and saw this old, old woman looking in and she jumped with fright. Then she realised it was her own reflection.

The next day Hywel and I were invited to Ballywilliam, near Cloyne, to have lunch with Molly's oldest daughter Sally. After lunch we walked down the grassy boreen, overlooking the ocean, to a cluster of ruined cottages and barns. This stretch of coastline was the last unspoiled one in Europe, said Sally, stretching from Cobh to Ballycotton. As we stood there, the sea sparkling with a thousand lights, I fell in love with the spot and wanted to buy the ruins; but I learned that a wealthy art dealer had bought the property and planned to build a millionaire's house.

A year later the art dealer, now in financial difficulties, was prepared to sell the property for £18,000 – the exact amount I had in my savings account! And so it was that I bought a ruin with a view, facing south, at the southernmost tip of Ireland, with the ocean stretching from east to west. When the solicitor in Cork, who had not seen the property, asked, 'Who are your nearest neighbours at the front?' I had to pause for a moment before replying, 'I suppose the Falkland Islanders!'

But for Molly it would never have happened. I had never been to Ireland and never dreamed that one day Hywel and I would have a home there as well as in Wales.

Some months later we returned with our great friend Dennis Vickers, an architect, to inspect the ruin. As we drove down the lane towards the glinting ocean, we could see a yacht far out and three fishing boats beneath a blue sky streaked and swirled with cloud. Flying a few feet in front of the car, low down, almost as though leading us, a kestrel was rising and falling. Hywel and I looked at each and smiled. It was, we felt, a happy omen.

By breakfast the next morning Dennis had produced drawings of what we wanted, incorporating the main cottage with its adjacent barns to create an L-shaped building. There was a second cottage, to be converted later, where friends would be able to stay. Will Kenneally, our builder, arrived promptly at noon – a bearded giant with a broad smile and one broken tooth. I left Hywel and Dennis to discuss practicalities with him. Hywel stood, his pale blue shirt billowing, holding a long measuring tape while Dennis unrolled the other end and made notes. The wind blew hard making the telegraph wires sing.

We waved goodbye to Will and awaited his estimate. Apart from royalties for *Re:Joyce!*, an entertainment about Joyce Grenfell which I had written for Maureen Lipman, I had been commissioned to write *One Foot on the Stage*, the biography of the actor Richard Wilson, as well as a book for Element publishers entitled *Passages of the Soul: Ritual Today*. The proceeds from all these would enable the first stage of building work to go ahead.

Back in London, however, Hywel woke after a disturbed night, feeling the burden of the Irish property if we went ahead with it. 'I'm not strong inwardly,' he said. He had seen the death of several friends, including Roel, and, of course, on top of all this his own five-month scare about AIDS. I replied that if the thought of the house in Ireland continued to undermine him we should not go ahead. But I also reminded him how the sea invigorated him and was healing, which he acknowledged. 'I will just have to work through my anxiety,' he said. In the event, as photographs reveal, the whole Irish project became for him a rich creative challenge, deeply fulfilling.

A year later Hywel and I returned to Ballywilliam to

check on progress, Hywel having already been over once on his own to keep an eye on things. Roofs were now on, floors laid, windows going in. All was going ahead with amazing swiftness.

We called on Sally's husband, George Phipps, who was painting the windows of their cottage. We sat down to mugs of tea and listened to his stories:

My mother regarded me as the After-Thought, and my brother as the Thought. I was brought up by the cook, the parlour maid, the butler and the coachman: they taught me everything. I remember one day getting into trouble and my mother sent for me. I fled the house and bumped into the coachman who was carrying a bale of straw. 'Help!' I cried, and he plonked the bale of straw on top of me so that when my mother arrived, breathless, asking, 'Charlie, have you seen George?' he replied, 'Oh, yes, he went that way!' But I had to pay for it later!

A few months later we flew again to Cork and hired a car to drive to Ballywilliam. What a transformation! It was now a long, low L-shaped house. The whole interior, painted white, flowed from room to room and, by removing the ceilings to expose the roof internally, a greater height had been achieved. My studio at the far end, where I proposed to sleep and work, was like a small white-washed Greek church, with criss-crossing beams; and the large curved windows, which were Hywel's idea, made it feel like a different space from the rest of the house.

Hywel was in his element, hugely enjoying the creative challenge of Ballywilliam and loving its nearness to the sea. He was gradually acquiring more and more furniture from the auction rooms of Islington and elsewhere. He envisaged it all like a stage designer, down to the smallest detail: ordering curtains to be made of a heavy, lined, oatmeal coloured material; commissioning special lamps to be made; suggesting I bring my long pine table from Wales to use as a work surface.

Suddenly we were concerned to learn that Angela Lansbury had bought the twenty-three acre field next to us, which by law gave her permission to erect a house. She wrote to reassure us that she was only having a small crofter type cottage built and that we would not even see her chimneys. In the event it turned out to be a Hollywood version of a crofter's cottage, more like a Cotswold manor house!

Over the months Hywel had been storing the furniture, lamps, curtains and bedding in our barn at the Old Rectory, and the day came when, accompanied by our friend Alexander Robertson, he was to set forth in a hired lorry to take it all over on the ferry to Ireland. By the time he had carried everything out of storage, the furniture stretched in a line from the barn to our double gates, like some gigantic open-air auction. When the van he had ordered arrived it was nowhere near large enough to accommodate everything. Suddenly, like guardian angels swooping down when needed, some passing cyclists stopped, asked what the problem was, and then took over. By wedging shapes together they managed to pack in far more than we had been able to do. But it still left a lot behind and Hywel was distressed not to have managed it all in one trip.

And so, a month later, he and I set forth from Bleddfa, this time in a small red van crammed higgledy-piggledy with the remains of the furniture, feeling like tinkers. We drove for three hours to Fishguard, followed by a three-and-a-half-hour crossing on the ferry, then another three hours of driving before arriving at Ballywilliam after sunset.

Hywel would not let me go inside until it was all furnished exactly as he had envisaged it. And when finally I entered I wept because it was so beautiful in its Shaker-like simplicity. He had planned every detail and the whole place expressed the essence of Hywel's being as well as of our whole life together. It was wonderful to be free of clutter. I had an immediate sense of being in a new phase of my life.

And yet I slept badly. So did Hywel, and eventually we talked this through. There was this underlying anxiety, as well as guilt, and a feeling of 'What have we done?' We now had three homes. Would we be for ever dislocated and divided in our loyalties to each? Yet we could not bear to use this place as a commercial venture, letting it out as a holiday home. It was too imbued with our own identities. Also I recognised that I had much to learn from this space. It was the hermitage I had always dreamed of. Hywel said, 'Even if we only have it for ten years, say, it will have been worth it.' Which indeed is what happened.

The garden was the next challenge, being just bare earth with a low stone wall separating it from a field that led down to the cliffs. I couldn't see what to do with it and once again it was Hywel who solved the problem. One morning, looking up from my writing table, I saw him carrying huge flat stones from the cliffs and laying them out in a large circle about fifteen feet in diameter. These, when cemented, became the focal point from which I designed paths and beds, like an Elizabethan garden.

On one visit we experienced a freak storm. The rain was hurled horizontally like thousands of fine needles, swiftly forming rivulets, streams and miniature lakes. The wind blew round the house like a cyclone, tugging at the tiles, and inducing in Hywel a deep depression as it reminded him of wet, cold days in their farmhouse in Llangynog. The wind was so relentless it gave us headaches. The waves rose thirty or forty feet, exploding against the rocks and leaping high into the air. There was thunder and lightning. All the ferries were cancelled. Hywel began to fear that it would be like this regularly.

Then, three days later, the storm blew itself out and we awoke to clear, rinsed skies and the sun shining. We walked for several miles along the beaches beyond Ballycroneen Sands, watching the waves unfolding in leisurely movements, while sanderlings ran about like clockwork toys. Gulls, ranked in their hundreds, motion-less, their backs to the sea, would suddenly take off into flight, whirling into the sky, before settling on another part of the beach. Hywel's love of this place was at once renewed and the storm seen in perspective.

The sculptor Ken Thompson arrived with a large slab of slate on which he had carved some lines from Wordsworth and which was fixed on the outside wall of my studio:

Our souls have sight of that immortal sea which brought us hither

Sometimes at night the skies were brilliant with stars. Over the darkened ocean myriad tiny lights would shine like glow-worms from small fishing boats while, further off, the lighthouse at Kinsale Point flashed its signals. I recall how, one August, Hywel and I carried out blankets and cushions onto his stone circle and lay there watching the Shower of Perseus, as scores of stars swooped and fell through the night sky.

Always when we drove into Midleton, our shopping town, even if we had been away for several months, the girls in the bank would look up from behind the counter, smile and say 'Welcome home!' I remember the first time we went shopping. It was the Feast of Corpus Christi and in the morning there had been the traditional procession of the Blessed Sacrament through the town. By the time we arrived, however, the streets were deserted. Every shop window had been decorated for the occasion, some with statues of the Blessed Virgin Mary and floral displays, some with statues of the Sacred Heart. The one that most intrigued us was a butcher's shop where legs of lamb hung from racks. In the centre was a plaster statue of Jesus as the Good Shepherd and a sign saying, 'Behold the Lamb of God'!

In any relationship there develops a partnership and sharing of tasks. Hywel was by nature neat and tidy and taught me to be so too. Because we were in an attic flat, above an elderly woman, he would also say 'Light on your feet!' as our floorboards were so creaky. Once a week he would go down on his hands and knees to wash the white tiles of the centre room. Everything had its proper place. My chief contribution was to cook our meals, whereas Hywel described himself as 'a food arranger'.

All my life I have been the cook; but once, when our dear friend Joyce Grant was staying with us in Ireland, I said, 'I'm fed up with cooking! I propose a rota: I will cook on Monday, Joyce on Tuesday, Hywel on Wednesday – and so on.' All went according to plan until Wednesday, when Hywel suggested with an insouciant smile, 'Let's eat out tonight!' And so I returned to my destined role as Martha!

Over the years many friends came to stay, and we had some wonderful times together. Having three homes was, however, an emotional as well as financial strain. I remember George Phipps ringing me once in London, saying in his deep growling voice, 'Jimmie, 174 tiles have just blown off your roof!' Also, because of the salt from the sea, both houses had to be repainted every year. Hywel was to be proved right when he said, 'If we have it for ten years that will have been a privilege,' and so eventually we had to let go of it. To this day I still hear the sound of the sea beating on the rocks, and miss its deep solitude.

Back in Wales we also sold the Old Rectory as being

too large for our needs, and Hywel found a small shoot-ing lodge, dated 1838, a few miles away on the Stanage Estate in the hills between Knighton and Presteigne. My heart sank when I first saw it: it was small with plas-tic windows that pivoted outwards, a pokey kitchen, a minute bathroom, and a steep field for a garden. 'Trust me,' Hywel said. 'It has potential.' He was indeed proved right. Over the first few years it trebled in size, provid-ing a sitting-cum-dining room, a downstairs shower and toilet, plus an extra bedroom and bathroom for guests. The tumble-down pigsty at the top of the garden, was converted into a handsome studio, and the steep field was transformed into two lawns linked by flights of stone steps. In the lower garden we built an octagonal sum-mer house and constructed an ornamental pool with a fountain. We also bought the four-acre meadow in front of us so that nothing could be built on it and spoil the magnificent view of the Clee Hill in the distance. And Hywel, who had a passion for trees, having been left some money by a friend, planted ten tall saplings in the meadow alongside the lane.

∼ 14 ∼

IN 1998 while Hywel was on holiday in India, I was diagnosed with cancer of the thyroid. The surgeon told me that I might lose my voice as a result of the operation. One night I awoke in a sweat of fear, only to hear an inner voice saying, 'You have an angel working alongside you,' and at once a calm descended on me, so that when Hywel returned from India and I broke the news to him, the fact that I was calm helped him.

I also wrote a letter, which I never sent him, in case I did not recover from the operation:

Dearest Hywel,

Just in case anything goes wrong and I don't come round from the operation I want you to have some word from me. I always marvel at the way we were given to each other, as though some special destiny were at work. Who is to tell? And though there have been occasions when, through my selfishness, I have caused you deep pain, I know that you have long forgiven me.

I know that if you were to die before me I would find it deeply painful and lonely, and yet I know, should that happen, that I would grow through the experience. And I hope that, should I go first, you too will grow through the loss of my physical presence. What is important to remember is what Tristram Beresford once said to me, 'The best of us is hidden away in other lives.' Those who meet me, whether they are aware of it or not, meet you in me, and I do not doubt that those who meet you find me in you. How could it be otherwise! This is why I love Sir Philip Sidney's poem which I always associate with you:

My true love hath my heart, and I have his,
By just exchange, one for the other given.
I hold his dear, and mine he cannot miss:
There never was a better bargain driven.

I think often of the journey I once made by boat to Hydra when I was directing *Oedipus* at Athens, and you had gone ahead of me for the weekend. As the sun set, there was the perfume of cypresses and herbs as the boat journeyed between the islands, and as the sky darkened the first stars appeared. There was the excitement of seeing Hydra and knowing that you were there, waiting for me: 'Journeys end in lovers meeting'. And there you were on the quayside, among the jostling crowd, laughing, with glowing eyes.

Dearest Hywel, we have so many rich and amazing memories. We have shared so much, learned so much from each other, and nothing, not even death, can take that away. The other day, going through my old journals, I came across the following extract when I was at the University of the South in Sewanee, Tennessee.

Always on these trips away I find myself thinking about Hywel who is the centre of my being. Whenever my thoughts turn to him they bring a sense of peace and squareness, as of everything being in its proper place. There is no one else. He is so essential, so fundamental a part of my being, and yet not in any narcissistic way. We are both too independent for that.

If I do die first you will be taken care of at every level of your being. I come back, as so often, to some words Tristram Beresford wrote after the death of a very close friend. The poem is called '*A Communication*', and ends with these words:

> Beckoned and buoyed by love, I go.
> The place I go to I will build for you.
> You hear me? I must leave now. It is now.

Dearest Hywel – I love you now and always shall. Thank you for your love, Jimmie

The thyroid was successfully removed. I didn't lose my voice. Hywel drove me to Wales to recuperate and stayed with me for several weeks. When we drove to Ludlow for him to get the train back to London, I said, 'Thank you for all your support,' and he reached out with his left hand, while still driving, to hold my right hand. Later that evening he rang from London to say, 'When you said in the car "Thank you for all your support", I meant to say something and I didn't. So I say it now – It's because I love you.'

I marvel still at how we were entrusted to one another in this relationship of love all those years ago. Being 'in love' is heady and exciting in the first years, but learning to love goes deeper and lasts longer. Can it have been by chance that we met? No, said Hywel, it was meant to be.

Andrew Sullivan in his book, *Love Undetectable,* claims that love is possessive, unlike friendship. But this seems to me an artificial definition. Love grows and takes on many colours: it is friendship rooted in openness. Hywel and I had grown through each other and our love was not self-enclosing but always reached out to include others. And our home at Waterloo Lodge, as with each of our homes, was an image of that love, something created by us both. Which is why on one of Hywel's birthdays I had our initials carved on the lintel above the porch: *H* and *J.*

Often, when I was at the Lodge on my own, I would wake two or three times in the night, and although I knew Hywel was in London it was as though he were asleep in his own bedroom in the Lodge, and I felt enveloped by his presence and safe.

≈ *15* ≈

MOMENTS FROM MY JOURNAL

≈ ≈

Hywel takes me to Somerset House to watch the fountain display. There is an avenue of fountains which rise and fall like trees made from spun glass, down which couples walk as though in a church, or children play hide-and-wet with their parents. A man of fifty, who looks like a civil servant, rides a tandem between the jets, along with his Malaysian wife. A small boy in a yellow bathing slip runs excitedly in and out of the fountains, placing a foot on a jet to hold the water down and then releasing it with shrieks of laughter as the power of the water splashes him.

≈ ≈

Hywel and I have been at Waterloo Lodge for a whole week and I do so love it when he can be here, there is so much sharing. He says, 'I want to show you the necklace,' and together we walk up the lane and through the gate into the top meadow where we sit on a bench we have made and watch the sun set. There, encircling us, is a line of hawthorn trees thick with blossom as though there has been a heavy fall of snow, and everywhere the sweet, rich scent.

Hywel loves going off on his own, discovering new things and places, then saying, 'Jump in the car, I am going to take you somewhere!' It might be to a wood with a deep carpet of bluebells, an old building or, as so often in London, to undiscovered parts of the city.

At a quarter to nine I hear the clip-clop of Hywel's feet going downstairs, then the sound of him raking out the ashes in the room below and laying the fire for the evening. Today we open the new season at the Bleddfa Centre. Few people will ever know how much he has contributed to the work of the Bleddfa Trust.

Walking in the woods at twilight, in the misted green darkness, we listen to the pheasants, noisy with their rattling alarums, like town-criers, as they settle to roost. Hywel's white birch is in leaf and the magnolia stellata in flower. The woods are full of bluebells and wild garlic, and the hedges crowded with forget-me-nots, stitchwort, herb robert, red campion, and the white flowers of the dead nettle.

∾ 16 ∾

IN A rehearsal of David Hare's play, *The Judas Kiss*, the young actor Freddie Fox, who played Lord Alfred Douglas, is reported to have said to Rupert Everett, who was playing Oscar Wilde, 'Could you not look at me more in that scene?' to which Rupert Everett replied, 'No, they are like an old married couple; they no longer look at one another, they take each other for granted.'

It is true that in many marriages and relationships this can happen – but not always. I can think of many exceptions. I recall Malcolm and Kitty Muggeridge in their old age and in spite of his earlier infidelities, seated across from each other at the table, their hands clasped. You could sense how close they were. And so it was in my relationship with Hywel. One arrives at a certain plateau which seems to go on for ever. I think what helped to strengthen our relationship over the years was that we learned to have times apart from each other. As Virginia Woolf writes, 'Human beings do not go hand in hand the whole stretch of the way. There is a virgin forest in each: a snowfield where even the print of birds' feet is unknown. Here we go alone.'

Hywel and I also valued periods of silence, times when it felt there was no need to talk. And always for him his hour-long walk on his own each day was, as he once said, his way of meditating. All this was in contrast to his social side which thrived in company, loving the dinner parties we used to give when he would tell some of his favourite stories. Often I would be in the kitchen serving up the next course when I would hear gales of laughter coming from the dining room. And then, needing help, I would call out 'Blodwen!' and Hywel would come running through. This nickname came about when once we were staying with Molly Keane. I was helping her in the kitchen and she asked Hywel to lay the table. A few minutes later she came in to me, saying 'That Blodwen doesn't know how to lay a table, she will have to go in the morning, and I shan't give her a reference!'

One of Hywel's favourite stories, which he told to perfection, had first been related to him by Helen Higham, wife of the literary agent, David Higham. She used to come to Hywel for Alexander lessons. Once a year, in their handsome house in Keats Grove, they would hold a soirée to which many of David's distinguished clients would be invited, one of whom was Dame Edith Sitwell who was his near neighbour in Hampstead. At about five o'clock the front doorbell rang and little Matthew Higham, then about nine, ran to answer. Standing on the doorstep was Dame Edith's chauffeur who had come to collect her. Running back into the room where Dame Edith was holding court, Matthew cried out, 'Dame Edith, you've got to go now!'

She looked at him and then said, 'Matthew, the next time I have a soirée you must come to it. There will, I am sure, be a number of people I shall want you to say that to!'

∼ 17 ∼

IN THE autumn of 2010 I began to notice that both Hywel and I were climbing more slowly the seventy-two stairs to our attic flat in Belsize Park Gardens, so I suggested that it would make more sense if we moved to a ground floor flat in the same area. This then led to a discussion about our home in Wales. There was never any question of either of us retiring to Wales since we both planned to go on working. So we decided to put both Waterloo Lodge and our flat on the market. They sold quickly and in October 2011 we moved into our new ground floor home half a mile away. On my birthday Hywel wrote in his card to me, 'Dearest, we have achieved the big leap and you've achieved your happy, happy 84th. As always, much LOVE, Hywel.'

Significantly, this was written in block capitals and not in his usual handwriting. And it was only a few weeks after moving in, that one day I observed him walking slowly, shuffling like a very old man. He also had difficulty in co-ordinating certain activities: for instance, he became distressed that he could no longer remember how to fix his tie. Then one morning I became aware that he had been in the bath rather a long time so I went in to see what was happening. He was sitting there, unable to move or speak, and when I went to try and lift him he was like a dead weight. I struggled and eventually got him out. He had had a seizure. Some two years previous to this he had had a stroke that lasted about ten minutes and he had been rushed to A and E, where a shadow was diagnosed on his brain. Now he was sent for an immediate brain scan and the specialist reported that it had grown into a tumour, albeit benign, but owing to his age, seventy-five, she was not prepared to operate. The sole form of treatment, the so-called Cyber-Knife – an electrically controlled form of radiation – was only available privately. I agreed that we should pursue this and draw from our savings. Hywel then went into the London Clinic for three sessions.

Much of the time Hywel would sit quietly, reading, his face grave. And yet, whenever our eyes met, he would smile and there was such sweetness in his expression. He became as trusting as a child. In the mornings when he took his bath, I would get him to kneel rather than sit, as this was an easier way of getting him out, and I would wash his bottom and back, like a mother washing her baby.

A close friend, whose husband had a rare form of Parkinson's Disease, wrote:

It was a joy to be with you both in your new home, the latest, and most probably the last, in a series of truly wonderful places you have created together. Though not as 'together' as previously because of Hywel's tumour, I could feel the serenity in him that you told me about. He seems to be in a good place, both internally and externally, surrounded by beauty. And the objects that are precious to you both, and the love of friends, and, most of all, your love. But there can be no doubt in my mind that this is hard for you who carry the anxieties and the stresses and sense of loss. Hywel is a beloved burden, but at times it may feel lonely and heavy for you. I remember sitting with you in your summer house at Waterloo Lodge in Wales where we talked about Tom's illness. You asked me whether I had the strength for what was to come. I said 'yes', not knowing what was involved. But I know you have that strength.

Hywel was increasingly unsteady on his feet, inclined to stagger from side to side. Having been a great walker all his life he was clearly shaken by this. He also got confused with words, could not remember his PIN number, and had to give up driving. Then one night I woke up to find all the lights on. It was 1:30. I saw his bedroom door open and he was standing there, fully dressed, convinced it was morning. When I said it was the middle of the night he argued fiercely that it wasn't, until I told him to look out of the window. I suggested he should get undressed and go back to bed but, in trying to get out of his ski pants, he fell and couldn't get up and he was too heavy for me to lift. I dialled 999. For the next two hours his body was shaking and he vomited frequently. The ambulance men also pointed out the many bruises on his body: clearly he had had more falls than he had let on about.

April 21st
Hywel falls in the garden and cannot get up.

April 22nd
Hywel falls in the street and cuts his hand.

April 23rd
Late in the evening I hear a loud thud. Hywel has fallen in the passage-way and badly bruised his hip.

April 24th
Hywel feels so unsure of walking this morning that I persuade him to stay in bed. I e-mail the consultant who asks me to bring him in at 1:30 today.

Another scan was taken. The Cyber-Knife treatment had stopped the tumour replicating; but what this latest scan revealed was a leakage of fluid into the brain. There was no medication that could cure this, said Dr Murphy the consultant, and it was this that was affecting his memory, his mobility and his urinary tract. The only treatment, she said, was a minor operation to insert a tube into the brain that would drain off the fluid through the abdomen. Because she could not risk Hywel having another fall she said, 'I have already booked a bed for him, and the operation will take place two days from now.'

Two days later I went to the Royal Free Hospital and waited from 4 p.m. to 7 p.m. until Hywel was brought back from the operating theatre. When he opened his eyes he gave a great smile to see me sitting there.

A week later he was physically and mentally more alert but convinced he was in a private hospital and kept asking how much it was costing!

It was then that a letter arrived, addressed to us both, from Jim O'Neill, a psychotherapist, a practising Buddhist and partner of the biographer Peter J. Conradi, which evoked such strong, shared memories of our life in Wales:

Dear James and Hywel,

I wanted to be in touch at this challenging time for you both in order to express my solidarity and also my deep appreciation for the kindness and warmth of friendship you have shown me over the few short years we have known each other. You seemed to have slipped away so inconspicuously and elegantly from our lives in Radnorshire. I have such fond and happy memories of the evenings and afternoon parties spent with you both at Waterloo Lodge and will always treasure the memory of Hywel standing at your gate in greeting. I am sure everyone who came to visit you was as charmed and made to feel as special as you made me feel on those visits. Those Christmases with the tree magically lit with candles and us standing round it, holding hands, and the personally chosen gifts, and of course the wonderful food, were for me, as I am sure they were for all your friends, joyous and heart-breaking at the same time: joyous because such fun and heart-breaking as they were such powerful reminders to cherish each passing moment and to keep friends close.

I pray that Hywel will quickly recover from this frightening illness and that you both have more time together in your new home. I also pray that you both can rest in the certain knowledge that whatever happens you know that having you both in our lives has been a huge and profound gift of love to all your friends. My love to you both.

Because the first shunt was not successful Hywel had to have a second operation. Finally, after three months in the Royal Free Hospital, where I would visit him daily, he was moved to the St Pancras Rehab Centre. There I met Dr Mufti who was in charge of him on a day-to-day basis. She explained that while the Cyber-Knife treatment had stopped the tumour replicating, nonetheless, a menigioma went on growing, albeit slowly. Hywel could live for several years, she said, and die of something quite different. On the other hand, it could all speed up and he might not have long to live. No one, she said, could predict the outcome and so she asked me if we would like to have the back-up of palliative care. I expressed gratitude for such support.

Hywel's sister Mair and I had a meeting with the team handling Hywel's case. The prognosis was not encouraging. He had deteriorated rapidly since first being admitted to St Pancras and even he was aware of this. Walking along a corridor, with me holding his arm tightly, he said, 'My balance isn't as good as it was, is it?'

Already there was a nurse sitting with him day and night in case he suddenly got up and fell – there had been several such falls recently. He was also doubly incontinent and disorientated, requiring assistance for all personal care tasks.

Saturday, June 23rd

I spend four hours at St Pancras. When Mair arrives with one of her daughters, Hywel does not recognise either them or me, he just stares at us. I sit opposite him and we gaze into each other's eyes, holding hands, for a long, long time. He seems to be looking from far away as though in another country. There is, for the very first time, a haunted look in his eyes, not understanding what is happening to him. I hold his gaze steadily by way of reassurance for there aren't any words. There is only love. Just by my being there he knows he is not alone. Once he tries to speak and I cannot understand what he is trying to say. Has he had another stroke?

Hywel was brought home in an ambulance and transferred in a wheel chair. He could not walk or stand and had to be lifted onto the bed. Camden Council supplied a hospital bed, as well as a nurse once a day, an all-night carer and four visits a day from two carers who washed and changed the bed linen. Camden's palliative team also visited.

Everything gathered momentum quickly. Except for his right arm Hywel was unable to move, was incontinent, and had to be spoon fed. He was now totally dependent on me to feed him, and on the carers to wash and shave him, change his pads and linen. I didn't find it easy giving him his complicated medications, some of which had to be crushed, as he had difficulty in swallowing. Occasionally he would make a sound but he had lost the power and the ability to speak. He was on a solitary journey and all one could do was be totally 'present'. Sometimes he would lie with his eyes open, fixed on a point ahead of him, his right arm stretching forward, a grave and urgent expression on his face, as he pointed forward and upwards with increasing urgency: what, or who, was he seeing? Were there others waiting ahead for him?

During these last months it was as though Hywel was becoming pure essence. A light seemed to shine from within him; there was a deep serenity as well as the trust-ingness of a child. The essence of who he was seemed to shine like a lantern in the darkness.

It being the first Sunday in the month, our meditation group assembled as usual. Formed in 2006, at the sugges-tion of our friend Celia Read, it was Hywel's task, after my short introduction, to strike the large Tibetan sing-ing bowl to signal the start of the meditation, its sound resonating for a full minute, and then thirty minutes later to signal the end of the meditation. Today his sister Mair, and Flomi her daughter-in-law, sat with Hywel in his bedroom while we gathered in the main room. I car-ried the singing bowl into his room and placed it on his bed. With his right hand he managed to strike the bowl, albeit very feebly, and everyone in the next room heard the circles of sound resonating.

The next day Celia e-mailed me:

I think of you both, and the peace and beauty and security that encircles Hywel and the many, many circles of love and support that surround you both and also all that you are pondering in your heart. It was such a powerful meeting yesterday and I felt very privileged to be part of it and that special time in your and Hywel's home, as the sounding of his gong grows softer, harder to hear, but will always resonate in ever widening circles.

June 26th
Hywel is slowly slipping away. These past few hours he has been sleeping, and I cannot wake him to feed him. Yet we also have long stretches of just gazing at each other: those beautiful dark eyes full of such love, warmth and gaiety. Sometimes he tries to speak but either it is an inaudible whisper or simply sound.

It is now that the sense of loss begins to creep up on me: that those lips which I have so often kissed, that laughter which we have so often shared, and that deep silent companionship, will no longer be physically there. Always, over the years, we have stopped two or three times a day, when passing each other, to embrace and kiss … and increasingly so in the past eighteen months he would pause for such an embrace, almost as though unconsciously sensing something was at work in him which he did not fully understand.

I am reminded of John Bowlby's work with children. He writes of how the primary need to be cuddled, when satisfied, forms the foundation of what Erik Erikson called 'the child's basic trust'. It is a need which persists in adult life. When held, one experiences security, protection and comfort. Holding is a gesture which has enormous therapeutic potency in the treatment of pain and despair.'

My prayer is that Hywel may die without pain, without too much anguish. Each dying, each death, however, is unique and all one can do is to keep watch and be present.

June 29th
Today Hywel's eyes are clear, gazing into mine for long periods.

July 7th
The palliative team who came today think that Hywel is likely to die within the next twenty-four hours. He doesn't recognise anyone and his breathing is very shallow. He may just make his seventy-sixth birthday tomorrow but he won't be going into the garden to see it all in bloom as I had planned. I am so deeply grateful that he is able to die at home.

Celia Read writes, 'How hard to believe that Hywel really is about to go on ahead without you, leaving you to follow him, you the one who has promises to keep and far to go before he sleeps. But such a relationship as yours will continue, cannot end. I had hoped that when he came home he would share this summer together in your beautiful home and life. But that was not to be. I think your image of being surrounded by many different circles is very important.'

Sunday 8 July 2012 was Hywel's birthday. I had invited a few friends to a birthday tea. Jonathan, our GP and friend, said the end was very near. One by one they all went into Hywel's room to say goodbye. Later that evening he died peacefully.

～ *18* ～

THERE WAS a book, published in the 1890s, which provided samples of letters for all occasions: from thanking someone for a gift, to sending greetings on the birth of a child, or expressing sympathy at someone's illness, as well as samples of letters of condolence to someone recently bereaved. Such things are no longer taught in schools and few people send hand-written letters any more. Letters of condolence are perhaps the most challenging of all: one doesn't want to gush or be sentimental, and yet how to strike the right note is often far from easy. This is why I have included here some of the letters friends and pupils wrote after Hywel's death, for not only do they reflect how he affected others, but they were also a rich support to me at such a time.

From Virginia Brownlow, in Ardmore:

Dear Jimmie,

Kevin phoned to tell me that Hywel had died. The tide was out. The beach I was walking on was vast, simple and lonely. It felt appropriate to hear the news there. I felt a big sense of loss, but also a great deal of gratitude for our friendship. I know I have lost a good person who used to look out for me – literally – he often looked out from your attic windows to ours across the street to see if the light was on.

Whenever I met him in the street my spirits lifted. That is a rare gift to give to a friend, and such a valuable one. I am so glad I met you the last time I saw Hywel in hospital. It made me so happy that you and he had such a relationship, and that he had such love and cherishing from you. You seemed calm, strong and realistic. I thought how held Hywel must have felt by your love. Maybe there's no other time in one's life when one is more in need of feeling truly held. I don't think I can imagine what it must feel like for you to be without Hywel after so many years together. I think a good deal about it. With love and sympathy.

From Sally Phipps:

My dear Jimmie,

My heart has been full of thoughts of Hywel since we got the news. He was a true original. I don't think I have met anyone else who was such a felicitous blend of delicacy and robustness. He was so funny and his remarks were delightfully perceptive, expressed in his lovely, light, witty voice. He was a wonderful teacher of the Alexander Technique and he must have helped many people with that – I think especially of his humour and kindness. I always remember Virginia coming in one day and saying, 'I have just met Hywel in the shop at Churchtown South. He was helping a blind man choose a hot water bottle.'

I always greatly admired the relationship between you two. It seemed to me to be so full of equilibrium and love and enjoyment. I congratulate the two of you for that. It is a marvellous achievement and must bring you strength at this very hard time of loss and change. I am praying for you.

Much love from George and me, Sally.

From Celia Read:

Such a death as you were able to share with Hywel has an intimacy and a generosity and physicality that makes it feel very close to a birth. It is the birth of a new stage in the journey of love. But a love without his dear lips to kiss and be kissed by, his body to hug and be hugged by; learning to live with these losses will take time and be painful. You are surrounded by love but still walk this journey alone, suffering the pain of missing his physical presence, his being there every day and in every way, the two of you entwined as you grew together. But you are now on your journey towards the discovery of his presence within you and all around you in a way that will never die.

Thank you for sharing all this with me and I know it will help me when Tom dies. With love, Celia

~ ~

And so I began to compose the order of the funeral service at St Mary's, Primrose Hill in London. The church was packed, with many friends travelling from Cornwall, Scotland, Wales, Oxford, as well as about a dozen of Hywel's colleagues from the Royal Opera House where he had worked in various productions, both operas and ballets, for over forty years.

The coffin was already in place as people arrived, flanked by six eight-foot tall olive trees in large pots, three on each side. There were no flowers on the coffin, only a simple wreath of olive twigs encircling a lit candle. The sun shone through the windows of the great white space of this handsome church, while a recording was played of Rosalyn Tureck performing Bach's *Goldberg Variations*, which Hywel and I had heard her play so long ago in the Festival Hall.

Marjorie Brown, the Vicar, began the service with these words:

> While we gather here to say goodbye, more than anything we celebrate the harvest of a rich and generous life which nourished so many people at different levels. And most of all we celebrate the remarkable love and friendship over fifty-four years of Hywel and James. As St Bernard of Clairvaux wrote on the death of his brother, 'I weep because of you, not over you. Our love had created a presence, one to the other. In truth, we were of one heart, one spirit – there was a unity of soul.'

There followed various readings, a hymn, and Marjorie Brown spoke of Hywel's great love of trees and how one friend had had one hundred trees planted in memory of him, in a new forest being created in Scotland. We then listened to a recording of Bryn Terfel singing Handel's aria, including the line 'Where'er you walk, trees where you sit shall crowd into a shade.'

Towards the end came the Commendation and Committal, when Hywel's family, his two sisters, their husbands, and all his nephews and nieces and I, gathered round the coffin for the words:

> We are gathered here around the body of Hywel, all that is left of him, to pay our respects and to do justice to his life and death. Rather than his body we are left with his name which we speak now with reverence and affection.

At that moment the packed church echoed with the name of 'Hywel!'. And then, in the words of Prospero to Ariel, we all spoke the line,

> *To the elements be free, and fare thee well!*

The next stage of the journey

Seated at Newport Station, waiting for the connection to Ludlow, rain pouring down, I reflect on how often, over the years, Hywel and I have made this journey to Wales, carrying our own sandwiches and coffee. Now it seems strange to be travelling with him in the form of a heavy square box containing his ashes, knowing that his spirit is elsewhere. Seated in this grey room with a grey sky outside is like an image of death, a terminus, with people waiting to depart, or greet a new arrival.

Helped by my friends Irene and Dennis Vickers, I scatter Hywel's ashes in the orchard alongside the Barn Centre at Bleddfa where, one day, my ashes will also be scattered. The day is overcast, but, just as we begin, the sun explodes, lighting up the countryside, and suddenly a blackbird begins to sing, and then all the birds, as we cover the orchard with fine white powder.

It was only then that the loss of Hywel began to hit me. As Jim Fitzgerald wrote to me, 'We are opened up to the depths of the soul by the death of a loved one.' But I did not weep, nor was I filled with self pity. It was, quite simply, work to be done, knowing that out of dying a new birth would come. Hywel was now blessedly free. I was happy for him – he was essentially such a joyous person. And he was ready to depart. There was such a serenity about him and I know that he now continues on the next stage of his journey. And though he and I always assumed that I, being nine years older, would pre-decease him, there was a rightness in it being the other way round, so that I was there to support him on the last lap of his journey. The deeper the love, the deeper the pain, but that is always the next test, for each turn of the wheel has something to teach us. We must move forwards or else we drift back.

One night I dreamed that I was lying in a narrow truckle bed and that Hywel got in with me. He was bony, as when I first met him. He climbed in as though needing my comfort and support and yet, at the same time, comforting me. Was I in a dream or half-asleep? I lay comforted in my grief by Hywel lying alongside me and I thought of some lines from the ninth century, translated by Helen Waddell.

By day mine eyes, by night my soul desires thee.
Weary I lie alone.
Once in a dream, it seemed thou wert beside me;
O far beyond all dreams if thou wouldst come!

In the next dimension, beyond death, there are no bodies such as we are used to, and yet it is clear to me that we shall know each other even more deeply. In those last weeks of Hywel's life, as the power of speech and movement left him, we would gaze for long intervals into each other's eyes, not needing words.

I awoke one night in the small hours, wide awake, feeling Hywel's presence so strongly, the immediacy of his presence, his love and his laughter, filling the entire room, closer than close, that I said out aloud, at the top of my voice, 'Hywel, you are AMAZING!' I felt we were in a deep place of contact that transcended the physical.

Later I read the following in Sylvia Townsend Warner's journals, after the death of her companion, Valentine:

Sept 30th
Waking from a dream of her I felt a kiss, the long imprint of a kiss above my right cheek. And the wind blew and the house was full of her presence.

Nov 27th
In a dream we stood side by side at her sitting-room,

watching a star appear and disappear in a web of cloud. And I said to her: I do love you so, and in a moment she clasped me in a living, solid embrace, her very arms about me. And I heard myself cry out, 'Valentine! Valentine! You are alive!' Life was there. We were alive again. And then her presence ebbed … but it was so real, so actual, that I lay with my body resounding with joy and felicity, warmed and kindled with the sensual reality of that embrace. Valentine! Valentine! You are alive!

Where do these experiences come from, many thousands of which have been recorded? Such visitations may emanate from our unconscious, being a form of self-healing, or they may be evidence of a continuing existence beyond this present one. I believe both are possible.

Although the pattern and rhythm of the life we shared was now broken and I was thrown back on myself, Hywel was never far away from me and I felt his presence very strongly. I knew I was not alone. Yet, at the same time, I had to learn to stand on my own feet: that was the challenge.

≈ ≈

A dream:

Hywel and I and others are in a large country house where we have been performing. I go for a long walk and lose track of time, so that when I return it is all over. People are packing up. The house is huge and I can't find Hywel anywhere, nor our car, and no one seems interested; they are all busy, packing to leave, and most of the cars have already gone. I search and search, asking people, 'Have you seen Hywel?' and yet I know I must stay at the centre and not wander off, for that would be hopeless. I reflect that he may have gone off in our car looking for me and if I stay here he will eventually return. I climb a slope, but there is a thick mist. In desperation I call out: 'Hywel! Hywel! Hywel!' I am really frightened now. And then I hear his voice, only a few feet away, closer than close, and I know that all is well. We embrace. Though I don't see him I know that he is there, and he holds me, and I know that he will always be there for me, as I was for him, and that I must never panic.

After sharing this dream with Celia Read, she wrote,

> This is indeed a big and important dream which will look after you; a dream of reunion, and Hywel's way of being with you, looking after you now. It shows that you have been able to create the internal space for him to inhabit. The relationship continues to cherish and inspire.

From Corfu our friend, the Jungian analyst Dr Anthony Stevens, wrote:

> I am touched by your experiences of being in such close relationship with dear Hywel. I am not surprised. You were such a symbiotic pair that the relationship could not possibly have ended with the death of one of you. I have, of course, been wondering about you and how you are surviving the loss of Hywel. A life-long

partner carries unlived and undeveloped parts of one's self. A positive way of living with loss, it seems to me, is to further the individuation quest by assuming responsibility in one's self for those unlived potentials in the here and now. Hard, but it adds a crucial significance to one's suffering.

As Stephen Segaller observes in *The Wisdom of the Dream*, 'In the wake of death the difficult psychological work continues. Death ends a physical life but not the psychological relationship which continues perhaps even more vividly in dreams.'

As I write it is now just over five years since Hywel died. I do not weep, and I have no doubt of his continuity in another existence. There are times when I feel him very close to me. Yet there remains, as with all who are bereaved, a deep sense of loneliness. The years of a shared life result in two people being able to sit comfortably in a room with no need to talk, each going about his own activities. Often Hywel would be in his favourite chair, deeply immersed in a book while I sat at my desk writing. Every now and then one of us would look up and smile. In the same way, moving about the flat, we would often stop to embrace. Deep down we all have a need to be held and embraced. Few people in life really hold one in this way.

Emily Dickinson writes, 'Loneliness is the maker of souls.' Loneliness is a common condition, even more so today. It can drive one to drink, drugs and sex, to constant noise and distraction. However, if one sits quietly, as in meditation, we can learn to face the resentments, angers, jealousies, feelings that come to the surface, to look at them and acknowledge them – to confront these darker aspects of one's self. It is interesting how at the beginning of Shakespeare's final play, *The Tempest*, Prospero calls Caliban 'a demi-demi devil!' but towards the end of the play he is able to say of him, 'This thing of darkness I acknowledge mine', whereupon Caliban replies, 'I'll be wise hereafter, and seek for grace.' Each of us has to learn how to confront our own inner fears, angers, shames – like St Francis of Assisi embracing the leper, or taming the wild wolf of Gubbio. Each of us has to confront the Minotaur within us and then ride it out of the labyrinth, harnessing its dark energy.

In my early twenties, when I was a devout Catholic, I used to serve Mass at the Carmelite Monastery in Golders Green. One day the Prioress showed me some photographs. One I recall was of an arch, painted above which were the words 'In Carmel and at the Judgement I am alone with God.' They were, and are, daunting words and yet a necessary reminder that each of us has to come to terms with this existential fact. People are often so afraid of loneliness that they will cling to terrible and even destructive relationships rather than risk letting go; yet there is no substitute for the courage to confront one's own inner loneliness. Unless we risk solitude we shall never hear the voice of wisdom within us. And in truth we are not alone for, as Joseph Campbell writes, 'One has only to know and trust and the ageless guardians will appear.' They may appear in one's dreams or in those individuals who suddenly come into our lives, quite unexpected, yet as though sent by some hidden command.

As I approach my ninetieth birthday I look back at a long avenue of friends: those who have at intervals appeared to point me in a certain direction, some who have travelled a long way with me and still do, and those who have had the courage to hold up a mirror to me so that I could see my faults and mistakes.

Some we may only meet once, as when, at the age of twenty-one, I happened to be passing a Catholic church in Ogle Street, in London, which I had never been to before. I decided to make my confession. The priest, after listening to me, suggested I go and see a certain Dr Elkisch in Gloucester Place. This was one of the most important turning points in my life for it resulted in the years of a rich Jungian analysis as a result of which Dr Franz Elkisch helped me assemble the pieces of my own jigsaw and reveal the person I was meant to be.

Today one sees so many marriages breaking apart, and children being damaged as a result. In any long-term relationship there will always be periods of loneliness when love seems to have died – but loneliness is essential to becoming a fuller human being. As Madeleine L'Engle has observed, we have only to persevere and the desert will flower again.

Epilogue

1956: a visit to Falls Cemetery in Virginia, USA

HERE PEOPLE are buried in neatly-mown green fields. There are no tombstones, just small plaques let into the ground. In the centre of this area the Swedish sculptor Carl Milles has designed a *Fountain of Faith*. In an oblong pool, with fountains shooting high into the air, figures in greened bronze stand on slender stems and, because of the way they are placed, seem to drift and float across the water like a moving pageant. Each figure is a portrait of someone known by the sculptor but now dead, yet imagined by Milles as meeting again after death.

A circle of young children, who were drowned at sea, race forward as on a beach, their faces upturned, eager and joyous, their hands outstretched. By them sits an old man looking up at the sky. A woman raises her hands in prayer. A boy, leaning his head meditatively on one hand, holds a lizard in the other, while a jackdaw perches on his shoulder. Nearby, a mother raises her new-born baby high in the air and a man comes forward to greet his wife with outstretched arms. Two sisters lovingly embrace and in a circle of lilies a boy walks shyly, holding a young bird in his hand while, high in the air, balanced on a tall flower, stands an angel, playing his flute, his head cocked attentively as though listening to the children at play below. The figures are seen silhouetted through the fine sprays of water, the sun dazzling and making a rainbow.

There is such a sense of joy and radiance, of journeys ending in lovers meeting, and I am reminded of some lines from Wordsworth:

> *Hence in a season of calm weather,*
> *Though inland far we be,*
> *Our souls have sight of that immortal sea*
> *Which brought us hither;*
> *Can in a moment travel thither*
> *And see the children sport upon the shore*
> *And hear the mighty waters rolling evermore.*

Acknowledgements

I would like to thank those friends who have read various drafts and encourged me to persevere in the sharing of my experience – Nicola Beauman, Norman Coates, Tony Morris, Kevin Trainor, and Lucy Fawcett at Sheil Land Associates who has so continuously supported me. I would also like to thank Dr Anthony Stevens who has helped me more than he realises, even though I was never a client of his, and whose friendship has deeply enriched my life.

Above all I want to thank Celia Read for her rare gift of friendship and insight as well as her ability to find the right words, which have proved so healing.

By the same author

Blue Remembered Hills: A Radnorshire Journey
Inner Journey: Outer Journey
Passages of the Soul: Ritual Today
Opening Doors and Windows: A Memoir in Four Acts
Finding Silence: 52 Meditations for Daily Living

BOOKS ON THE THEATRE
Directing a Play
Experimental Theatre
London Theatre: from the Globe to the National
One Foot on the Stage: The Biography of Richard Wilson
Darling Ma: The letters of Joyce Grenfell to her Mother
    (ed)
The Time of My Life: The Wartime Journals of Joyce
    Grenfell (ed)

STAGE ADAPTATIONS
Laurie Lee's *Cider with Rosie*
Helene Hanff's *84 Charing Cross Road*

CHILDREN'S BOOKS
The Adventures of Odd and Elsewhere
The Secret of the Seven Bright Shiners
Odd and the Great Bear
Elsewhere and the Gathering of the Clowns
The Return of the Great Bear
The Secret of Tippity-Witchet
The Lost Treasure of Wales

James writes a fortnightly blog of thoughts
and inspirations:

www.jamesrooseevans.co.uk

For information about
The Bleddfa Centre for the Creative Spirit
see:

www.bleddfacentre.org